J174

Fall of Eagles

*The end of the great
European dynasties*

John Elliot

D1423923

British Broadcasting Corporation

Published by
the British Broadcasting Corporation,
35 Marylebone High Street,
London W1M 4AA

ISBN 0 563 12470 9

First published 1974
© John Elliot 1974

Printed in England
by Jolly & Barber Ltd,
Rugby, Warwickshire.

Contents

The television series *Fall of Eagles* was first shown on BBC-1 between March and June 1974.

The main characters were played as follows:

Franz Josef	Laurence Naismith
Empress Elizabeth	Rachel Gurney
Archduchess Sophie	Pamela Brown
Andrassy	Sandor Eles
Aehrenthal	John Moffat
Wilhelm I	Maurice Denham
Fritz	Denis Lill
Vicky	Gemma Jones
Wilhelm II	Barry Foster
Bismarck	Curt Jurgens
Alexander III	Tony Jay
Empress Marie	Ursula Howells
Nicholas II	Charles Kay
Alexandra	Gayle Hunnicutt
Grand Duke Nicholas	John Phillips
Witte	Freddie Jones
Milyukov	David Collings
Stolypin	Frank Middlemass
Izvolsky	Peter Vaughan
Lenin	Patrick Stewart
Krupskaya	Lynn Farleigh
Trotsky	Michael Kitchen
Queen Victoria	Perlita Neilson and Mavis Edwards
Edward VII	Derek Francis

The scriptwriters were Keith Dewhurst, John Elliot, Trevor Griffith, Elizabeth Holford, Ken Hughes, Troy Kennedy Martin, Robert Muller, Jack Pulman, David Turner and Hugh Whitemore

Series created by John Elliot

Series producer Stuart Burge

Preface

The first purpose of this book has been to provide a background to the BBC Television drama series 'Fall of Eagles'. It may also, I hope, serve as a general introduction to a period of history which I have found fascinating, whether the reader sees the television series or not. The eagles which fall are the ruling houses of Austria, Russia and Germany, all of whose empires collapsed in 1918 after centuries of despotism, and the series traces their story from the middle of the nineteenth century. It is not itself a history, but a set of thirteen plays about the people mainly concerned. Its principal characters are the three emperors who were the dominant rulers of Europe during that time – Emperor Franz Josef of Austria, Kaiser Wilhelm II of Germany, and Tsar Nicholas II of Russia – and they are also the central figures in this book.

Empires are imposed on men by other men. Unless one believes in the Divine Right of Kings, there is no superhuman agency one can blame or praise for them; they are simply forms of society which mankind chose and then discarded with struggle and pain – in Europe as recently as our parents' and grandparents' day. To make a poetic comparison, an empire is like a flower on the tree of human life, which unfolds in glory, grows overblown and fragile, and falls of its own corruption when shaken.

As empires are essentially tribal arrangements, each revolves around a tribal chief, and as the chieftain begets an imperial family a curious dualism develops, in which royal family life becomes entwined with the fortunes of the nation. As time goes on, the members of the family which made the empire become the prisoners of it – symbols of an established *régime* in which their real power depends on a shifting balance of circumstances and personalities within a set form.

By the middle of the last century the great dynasties of Europe – Hapsburgs, Romanovs and Hohenzollerns – were as much the puppets of history as its creators, although they did not realise it – and their tragedy lay in that. In a sense, they were like film stars, in whose lives their subjects saw a grander reflection of their own destinies; theirs was the glory, the glamour and the wealth which commanded, apparently, whatever they desired. Their characters coloured and influenced what happened, often more than seemed sensible. But they had not written the plot. Here we are concerned only with the last two generations of these extraordinary people, or rather of these perhaps quite ordinary people caught at the centre of events. Any point of entry into their story is arbitrary, but a convenient one – and the one which we have chosen – is Vienna a century and a quarter ago.

A list of source works and further reading is given at the end of this book. I should also like to record my thanks to Elizabeth Holford who wrote some of the text, and to Dr Leslie Mitchell of University College, Oxford, for his generous advice, Miss Jennie Osborn for research, Mr Norman Higham, Librarian of Bristol University, for access to source material, Mrs Jan Doody for preparing the typescript, and the whole production team of the television series for their co-operation and enthusiasm.

J.E.

Europe Before 1914

GREAT BRITAIN

London

North Sea

NORWAY

SWEDEN

FINLAND

St.Petersburg

Baltic Sea

RUSSIAN EMPIRE

Moscow

DENMARK

SCHLESWIG HOLSTEIN

HOLLAND

BELGIUM

HANOVER

PRUSSIA

HESSE

GERMAN EMPIRE

SAXONY

Berlin

POLAND

GALICIA

Paris

FRANCE

SWITZERLAND

BADEN

WÜRTTEMBERG

BAVARIA

AUSTRIAN EMPIRE

Vienna

HUNGARY

ROUMANIA

CROATIA

BOSNIA

SERBIA

ALBANIA

BULGARIA

GREECE

CRIMEA

Black Sea

Constantinople

T U R K E Y

ITALY

SPAIN

Mediterranean Sea

Franz Josef in 1849

Chapter one

Franz Josef

In December 1848 Prince Franz Josef ascended the Imperial throne of Austria, in succession to his hopelessly dim-witted uncle Ferdinand, who had been persuaded to abdicate. The new Emperor was eighteen. The older man knelt before him, whispered, 'Be brave – God will protect you – it was done gladly', and shuffled out of the state rooms of Europe, taking with him the ghosts of the post-Napoleonic age.

Since the fall of Napoleon and the Congress of Vienna in 1815, Austria had been the diplomatic centre of an emperor-ridden and reactionary continent. The great fires of the French Revolution and the Napoleonic conquests had burnt out, and miraculously the old buildings remained. The kings had returned to their palaces, the etiquettes and regalia and social and political systems of the imperial past had been dusted and put back in place, and the Austrian Chancellor – foxy, unrelenting Metternich – had presided over Europe for thirty-three hidebound and spellbound years.

There were still fires in the cellars: the weight of autocratic rule presses hard on the masses underneath, and the sparks of repressed ideas make the material below combustible. In 1830 a few flames licked up and were put out, but not for long. In 1848 'all the smouldering grievances of the Continent suddenly flared up.'[1]* The year began with risings in Italy against Marshal

* The figures refer to the notes on p. 220.

Prince Metternich   *Louis Kossuth*

Radetzky's Austrian army of occupation; in February there was street fighting in Paris and King Louis Philippe – last of the Bourbons – abdicated; revolts broke out in Belgium, Holland and the independent states of the German Confederation, including Prussia; in March, in Budapest, the Hungarian revolutionary Kossuth demanded the abolition of serfdom and the end of absolute rule from Vienna.

The Austrian capital was still a medieval and baroque city, delightfully straddling the Danube, full of waltz-time and the sky-blue tunics of hussars. It must have been difficult for the Viennese to think seriously about the future until it burst on them in 1848. On 13 March street fighting began in Vienna itself and Metternich was dismissed. He was an old man: it was the end of his career and of his era. An independent government was set up in Budapest, and claimed to be tied to Vienna only by the Austrian Emperor, who was acknowledged as King of Hungary under what was to be called a Dual Monarchy. The Emperor Ferdinand – charming, epileptic and mentally unequal to the

Street-fighting in Vienna in 1848

situation – agreed, and insurrection continued. The Austrian Empire was now severely threatened, and the court fled to Innsbruck.

In Paris, however, the left wing was put down bloodily in the June Days; and the forces of counter-revolution began to organise themselves all over Europe. In August the working-class movement in Vienna was crushed and the Italian rebels defeated. In Austria the score was now one-all and everything depended on the final set – against Hungary. Clearly Ferdinand was not up to playing it, and he was persuaded to abdicate.

Franz Josef was not the heir: his father, Ferdinand's equally simple-minded and weak-willed younger brother, still lived, but his mother, Archduchess Sophie, was an intelligent, capable woman – known locally as the only man about the place – and was determined to restore the House of Hapsburg through the agency of her eldest son. She cleared the way for him, and on 2 December the slightly pop-eyed youth found himself on the throne. He was an unimaginative lad, but a worker, with fair looks, a good carriage and other promising, emperor-like qualities, among them obstinacy, stamina and a rather formal courtesy. Intellectually and politically, he was entirely under the thumb of his mother.

Since the thirteenth century the Hapsburg family had stood at the head of a vast assortment of territories and races – the legacy of the Holy Roman Empire – which now stretched from the Swiss border in the west to that of Russia in the east, and from Germany in the north deep to the south into Italy; but they stood, not as kings before their subjects, but as lords before their tenants. The emperor's lands were his estates: there was no sense of national unity between the ten million Germans and Magyars and the thirty million Slavs and other minorities whose bodies and souls Franz Josef inherited. They were his by the will of God, and he settled down conscientiously to govern them – the Hapsburgs were good Catholics.

His training had been in the army and his tastes – with one notable exception – were frugal and his ways austere. He slept in a soldier's bed beside a wooden camp washstand. He rose at dawn. His mind was as efficient and limited as a quartermaster's, his sense of protocol and authority absolute. His mother told him that his task was to restore and maintain order and discipline, and he devoted his life to it. His relaxations were music, hunting and reading the Army List. The exception to it all was his lifelong lechery; he was still capable of rape in his sixties, and in his youth his mother encouraged promiscuity to avoid the danger of an unsuitable permanent liaison. In all other circumstances he was remote: shy, sensitive, correct, polite, and unattainable. His first and only Prime Minister, Prince Felix zu Swarzenberg, wrote to the aged Metternich: 'The quality which is most valuable to him in his present position is his courage. Physically and morally he is fearless and I believe that the main reason why he can face the truth, however bitter, is that it does not frighten him.'

Franz Josef's imperial troops entered Hungary but the Hungarians fought them back with resolution and success; they were tired of being tenants, and winds of liberal nationalism were blowing through Europe. In the same month that Franz Josef came to the Austrian throne, Louis Napoleon, nephew of

Napoleon III

Napoleon Bonaparte, had been elected President of a new French Republic. This egotistical romantic became the whimsical champion of national liberation everywhere. He could do little for the Hungarians against Austria; but he began to help the Italians. So, out of the chaos of 1848 two men – an Austrian autocrat and a French adventurer – emerged to face each other and, between them, dominated Europe until the rise of Prussia nearly twenty years later.

Nicholas I

In a Europe of feudal Imperial estates, the anointed landlords maintained their own exclusive club, the Holy Alliance, and in 1849 Franz Josef invoked the aid of his fellow-member, the Tsar of Russia. Tsar Nicholas I had been watching Europe with some anxiety that its contagion might spread to his own considerable lands. Both duty and prudence inclined him to help the Emperor of Austria, and in May Russian armies were sent against Kossuth's Hungarians. At the same time the Austrian general

General Heynau

Julius Andrassy

Heynau – commonly known as General Hyena – was recalled from a savage pacification of Italy to help put down the Hungarians with similar brutality. Resistance ended in October. Kossuth and other Hungarian leaders – notably the 27-year-old Count Julius Andrassy, elegant, dashing, astute – fled. They were hanged in effigy and the President and thirteen generals executed, along with hundreds of others. The repression was without mercy. By the time Franz Josef was twenty-four he had signed about two thousand death warrants. But the Austrian Empire was saved. Central Vienna returned to its *gemütlich* life of opera, pastry shops, dance-halls and Johann Strauss, ringed with the tenements of the poor.

Franz Josef, in his twenties, was an enthusiastic dancer. Bismarck, who met him in 1852, wrote that 'he puts an excessive strain on his physical strength by dancing, riding and doing without sleep'; but, however late the night, Franzi was always up at 4.30 in the morning for a ten-hour stint at his desk, as though the problems of government were solvable by diligence alone. Understandably, he was not universally popular and when, in 1853, he was shot at it became clear that, wherever else he found his satisfactions, it was his duty to take a consort who might produce an heir. Naturally the choice was not left to him.

The Archduchess Sophie was herself the elder daughter of the King of Bavaria, and already had her eye on one of the daughters of her sister Ludovika. Ludovika had done less well for herself than Sophie, marrying a rather rakish Bavarian duke, Max Wittelsbach, who played the fiddle and tended to disappear into the Middle East disguised as an artist, returning with small negro boys. His advice to his daughters was that they should learn to move like angels with wings on their feet. Their second daughter, Elizabeth, was known as Sisi, the European royal families having a common predilection for daft nicknames. She was soon found to be regrettably like her father, and was allowed to roam free among the lakes and forests, the music and dreaming peace of a small European court. Sometimes he and she would sneak off together to fairs and country weddings disguised as strolling players, and entertain the locals. In 1853 she was fifteen, restless and imaginative – and very beautiful.

Sophie's eye, however, was on Sisi's elder sister, Hélène, who was slim and serious and, at nineteen, entirely suitable. Although Hélène and Franz Josef were first cousins, the Archduchess was undeterred by either the fatal dangers of inbreeding or the fact that the marriage would be against Canon Law: the Hapsburgs constantly intermarried and, as influential Catholics, could depend on the Pope to come up with a dispensation. In August she invited Ludovika and the two girls to the Imperial Palace of Bad Ischl, outside Vienna, and prepared Franzi to meet his intended; but Franz Josef immediately preferred Elizabeth, and said so.

The extraordinary accident of love at first sight seems all the more extraordinary in the career of this plodding roué. It is easy to believe that the very young Elizabeth was swept off her feet by the glamour and luxury of an Imperial court, but harder to understand how the Emperor, at twenty-three, could be so intemperately carried away. The infatuation lasted the rest of his life.

Contradicting his mother for the first recorded time, Franzi proposed to Elizabeth, showered her with presents – including a talking parrot – and married her the following April. In an attempt to teach her a little history, her father – with an endearing lack of political tact – appointed as her tutor a Hungarian,

Count Majlath, who induced in her a sympathetic understanding of the Magyar way of life. Poetic and persecuted gipsy horsemen were all she needed, as a lover of horses herself, to complete her romantic vision of adult life. It does not seem to have occurred to her that Hungary was her bridegroom's enemy.

There is nothing like a royal wedding to wash away memories of unrest, and the Viennese, who knew how to do these things, welcomed their charming and beautiful Empress with a *réclame* which echoed across Europe; even the London *Times* was sufficiently moved to report that she 'smiled and bowed to her future subjects as if every face on which her eye rested belonged to an old and valued friend', and Franz Josef, bathed in her reflected glory, declared himself 'as much in love as a lieutenant and as happy as a god'.

The morning after her wedding night she was required to get up and take breakfast with her mother-in-law as though nothing had happened. Possibly it had not: according to one account, the Emperor did not succeed with the Empress until the third night, whereupon the news had to be reported at once to the Archduchess. Although the relationship between Sisi and her Franzi remains mysterious and elusive, its key probably lies in the early nights and days of their marriage. Still only a girl, Sisi became virtually Sophie's prisoner, and grew to hate her, while her attitude to Franz Josef slowly hardened into a curious mixture of frigidity and affection. Sophie actually rather liked Elizabeth, but regarded her as inadequate and in need of training. Entombed in the most formal court in Europe, constantly corrected, lonely, the young Empress grew debilitated and touchy, like a caged animal. When, in the following year, she gave birth to a girl, the baby was named Sophie and removed to the Archduchess's apartments, to be brought up there. Elizabeth retired into gloom, wrote melancholy verse, and complained incessantly to Franz Josef, who had resumed the even tenor of his way.

He had plenty to preoccupy him. The Crimean War broke out in the year of his marriage, with British and French expeditionary forces attacking Russia's Black Sea coast. The beleaguered Russians, remembering their intervention in Hungary, expected the Austrians to help them in return, and when Franz Josef's government remained immovably neutral an iciness which was

Empress Elizabeth at the time of her marriage

never to thaw crept into relations between St Petersburg and Vienna. 'I am only sorry for the young Emperor,' the Russian ambassador observed, 'for his policy has wounded us Russians so deeply that he can be sure of not having another moment's peace so long as his reign lasts.' The isolation of the Hapsburgs had begun.

Franz Josef's concern was to patch up quarrels nearer home, particularly in Italy, which Cavour was looking to France to help unify at Austria's expense. The Austrians still occupied Lombardy, where they were hated; and Louis Napoleon, now Emperor of France, was feeling his way between the cold shoulders of European diplomacy with a killing in view, although only Bismarck – a cool observer in the Prussian *corps diplomatique* – guessed what he was at. 'France is now all velvet paws in Vienna,' he wrote in 1856, 'but the claws will soon be showing. His position, his character and his habits will all prevent Louis Napoleon from keeping the peace, and Italy lures him.'

As a gesture of conciliation to his unwilling subjects there, Franz Josef made a royal progress through northern Italy that winter and took Elizabeth with him. It was her first state visit and she was an unmitigated success: the Italians, who received their overlord without enthusiasm, found her *gentile,* and it is suggested that she did in fact soften and humanise the Emperor's attitude. Certainly some concessions were made; the iron grip of the Archduchess's policies began to loosen. The British Consul in Venice noted approvingly, 'Her Majesty's exquisite beauty, her grace and affability, have all contributed to win the sympathy and welcome of the masses'.

It was a small thing, but it helped Franz Josef, who decided on a repeat performance in Hungary in the spring, despite his mother's opposition and Sisi's reluctance. One of the many neuroses which Sisi was to develop during her life was a hatred of ceremonies, an unfortunate trait in her position. She complained that on ceremonial occasions she felt 'on show like a freak in a circus', and took to carrying a black fan to frustrate photographers. In all, she behaved increasingly like the spoilt child she was, her manner changing with her moods, either 'childishly naive or coldly distant'.[2] By now she had produced a

second daughter, Gisela, who was also whisked away into Sophie's quarters. In spite of all this, Franz Josef insisted on her company in Budapest, and when she named her price – that the two little girls should go with them, away from the Archduchess's care – that too was agreed.

To her surprise, Elizabeth enjoyed Budapest: Count Majlah's propaganda had done its work and she quickly found, in the vitality of Magyar life, the magic of a dream realised. The bravura, the music, the flowers and above all the horses were very much to her taste. As the people warmed to her she became more beautiful, graceful and affable than ever, for the admiration was mutual and the Hungarians realised that at last they had a friend at court. Her presence made even Franz Josef moderately acceptable, and her agency secured the pardon and return of the exiled Hungarian leaders, among them Julius Andrassy. It is possible that, even at this early stage, Andrassy thought of Elizabeth as a means of obtaining a measure of independence from Austria, but her attention was immediately diverted to other things: her elder daughter, Sophie, died in Budapest. Sisi was prostrated.

At the end of the tour they returned to Vienna, where Sisi submitted again to the royal will, and the following summer she gave birth to a son and heir, whom they called Rudolf. Franz Josef by now worshipped her, with a love which became more and more hopeless and obsessive. Emotionally and intellectually she remained always above him, just out of reach, as she grew into a bizarre, accomplished and ravishing woman. Her oval face, with its lovely brown eyes, was set in a glory of chestnut hair, long and heavy and shampooed with egg-yolks and brandy. Her mouth, turned up a little at the corners, was kept closed, hiding rather yellow teeth: she smiled but did not laugh. She had a morbid fear of growing fat and so dieted, becoming often unwell and melancholic. When she was well her energy was frightening: she would rise with her husband and walk or ride all morning at a prodigious rate, recapturing her childhood freedom. She sang and played the zither and became a pupil of Liszt. She loved the poets – Heine, Shakespeare, Byron, Lamartine – and translated some of them. Hasenauer, a contemporary scholar of some distinction, said of her, 'one needs a thorough knowledge of history, art and science to be able to converse with her, her learning is astonishing'. She wore simple clothes, with

The Austrian imperial family in 1860
Standing, left to right: Emperor Franz Josef, Archduke Ferdinand Maximilian (later Emperor of Mexico), his wife Archduchess Charlotte, Archduke Ludwig Victor, Archduke Karl Ludwig.
Sitting, left to right: Empress Elizabeth with Archduke Rudolf, Archduchess Gisela, Archduchess Sophie, and her husband Archduke Franz Karl, the Emperor's father.

chamois-leather underwear, fell in love with the sea – 'the ocean is like a mighty mother on whose breast one can forget everything' – and entirely filled one room in the Imperial palace of Schönbrunn with photographs and paintings of horses.

If, as seems certain, Sisi knew of Franzi's physical infidelities, she turned her back on them to live a life of her own. The Emperor, while prepared to gratify even her more extravagant whims, failed utterly to follow her devious and fantastic progress, and soon gave up the attempt. 'To Elizabeth he owed all he knew of personal happiness; to her, too, some of the darkest hours of his life';[3] but not all.

In 1859 Cavour provoked Austria into another war in Italy. This time the Italian liberationists were supported by Napoleon

The battle of Solferino. Above, Napoleon III; below, Franz Josef

III and a large French army. Franz Josef had no allies, and his troops, incompetently led and inadequately provisioned, were driven back and suffered at Magenta a defeat bloody enough to coin a new word for red. Leaving his desk for once, Franz Josef hurried to Italy to take personal command of his soldiers and, on 24 June, faced Napoleon at Solferino, where the opposing sovereigns stood 'at the head of two vast armies which neither knew how to command'. At the end of the day Franz Josef retired, leaving forty thousand Austrians dead and dying.

'My dear, my heavenly Sisi,' he wrote from the battlefield, 'my only, most beautiful Angel. I can't tell you how much I love you – how much I think about you. If you still love me, do not grieve so much. Fortune did not smile on us. I am the richer by many experiences and have learned what it feels like to be a defeated general.'

He was nothing if not resilient. He ceded Lombardy but kept Venetia and, returning to his desk in Vienna, sacked most of his ministers and set to work once more to rebuild his Empire on the ruins of the past, taking – with great caution – a new path. 'Now we are going to have a little parliamentarianism,' he told his mother, 'but all power stays in my hands.'

Chapter two

The English Marriage

Parliamentarianism, in mid-nineteenth-century Europe, was more honoured in the breach than in the observance. Prussia and other North German states possessed parliaments which had to vote taxes but otherwise had no real power. Holland, Belgium and the Scandinavian kingdoms had evolved into constitutional monarchies, which were looked on with pity by the entrenched Emperors. The Tsars had never contemplated a parliamentary experiment, and even France was an Empire again.

Of the major powers only Britain was a constitutional monarchy. Outside Europe Britain was the greatest power of all, with possessions which stretched from Canada to New Zealand and included India. Whether because Britons were more naturally democratic, or because they had got over their revolutions earlier, or merely because a succession of indifferent foreign monarchs had left an elected native government to speak for them, the result was that Queen Victoria was the only considerable Head of State who did not make laws. Her husband, Prince Albert of Saxe-Coburg-Gotha, was a German prince in the European liberal tradition. Victoria and her Prince Consort shared a common uncle, King Leopold of the Belgians, whose right and proper sentiments of sober enlightenment were offered generously to them both from their early childhood. Albert himself was a moral and serious young man: at sixteen he had

Queen Victoria and Prince Albert with the Prince of Wales in the early 1850s

Prince Albert in 1860

The royal family at Osborne in 1857
Left to right, Prince Alfred, the Prince Consort, Princess Helena, Princess Alice, Prince Arthur, the Queen with Princess Beatrice, Princess Victoria, Princess Louise, Prince Leopold and the Prince of Wales.

written a short *History of German Civilisation* which included 'a retrospect of the shortcomings of our time, with an appeal to everyone to correct those shortcomings in his own case, and thus set a good example to others'. With such origins and precepts behind them, it was not surprising that the British royal family found the political progress of Germany a cause close to their hearts.

Safe, rich and condescending, Victorian Britain had only one continental friend of any consequence, the France of Napoleon III, her ally in the Crimea. Russia was as unlikely to forgive the Crimean adventure as Austria Britain's undisguised sympathy with the Italian 'rebels'. Even the Prussians, in whose minds premonitions of future power were beginning to stir, resented the interference of the British queen and her Coburg relatives. But Albert was not deterred. Innocent and hard-working at home, designing improving frescoes, playing the organ at Windsor Castle, opening museums and hospitals and planning sewage-farms, he cherished one consuming extra-territorial ambition: that the confederated petty states of Germany should be combined into one constitutional kingdom, firmly linked by dynastic ties to the liberal destinies of Britain, for the moral salvation of Europe and the good of mankind generally; and he unwittingly sacrificed his favourite child to this end.

Vicky at the time of her marriage to   *Fritz Wilhelm*

On 2 September 1855 Queen Victoria wrote in confidence from Balmoral to Uncle Leopold in Belgium that '*Our* wishes on the subject of a future marriage for Vicky have been realised in the *most gratifying* and *satisfactory* manner'. The eldest child of the Queen and Prince Albert was not yet fifteen, but it had long been Albert's hope – and therefore Victoria's – that she should marry Fritz Wilhelm, the only son of the Prince of Prussia and eventual heir to the Prussian throne. Fritz's mother, Princess Augusta, shared Albert's liberal views and his dreams of a Germany united under a democratic Prussia. Her husband, whose views were less certain, had been exiled in England long enough after the 1848 revolution to receive a great deal of good advice from Albert on constitutional government.

Although Vicky was still in the schoolroom, Fritz was twenty-four that summer, and the time seemed ripe for an informal visit to the family in their Highland home. Fritz doubtless knew his duty and 'look'd to like'. After six days he told the delighted parents that 'finding Vicky so *allerliebste*, he could no longer delay making the proposal'. A few days later he was given his chance to 'speak' to Vicky as they rode their ponies over the moors together, and was rapturously accepted.

The wedding of Vicky and Fritz, 1857

The Prussian court expected the wedding to be in Berlin, but Victoria soon put a stop to that. 'The assumption of its being too much trouble for a Prince Royal of Prussia to come over to marry the Princess Royal of Great Britain in England is too absurd, to say the least,' she wrote. 'Whatever may be the usual practice of Prussian princes, it is not every day that one marries the eldest daughter of the Queen of England. The matter therefore must be considered as settled and closed.'

The marriage took place at the Chapel Royal of St James in January 1858, and Mendelssohn's Wedding March was played for the first time as the couple walked down the aisle between a great assemblage of royalty, British and foreign. The bride was just seventeen, small and still childishly round of face, her rather homely features enlivened by a warm smile and beautiful eyes. Vicky had inherited her mother's vitality and her father's good brain and enquiring mind. The two and a half years of her engagement had been spent in preparing herself under his guidance for her new role. She was well versed in German language and literature and the complexities of German history and politics. Although the Prince Consort felt the loss of his beloved 'Pussy', he was confident that she was fitted for her

Vicky

'somewhat difficult position'. Fritz Wilhelm – tall and fair with a promise of mature good looks – was pronounced by Queen Victoria 'a dear, excellent young man'. Though less quick-witted than Vicky, he was intelligent, a convinced liberal, and satisfactorily open to his father-in-law's advice. The future, for themselves and for Prussia, seemed promising.

A month later, in bitter weather, Fritz and his bride drove into Berlin. 'Every bit of me is frozen,' Vicky reportedly said, 'but my heart is warm.' The English princess was full of hope and high ideals, but within two weeks she was writing home, 'How my eyes have been opened'. Her text-book knowledge of Prussia had not prepared her for the realities of a cynical court, full of intrigue, and a society which glorified its army, deified its king, and was dominated by the narrow conservatism of the land-owning Junker class. From Paris Otto von Bismarck – still waiting in the wings – wrote, 'If the Princess can leave the Englishwoman at home, she may be a blessing to the country'; but that was exactly what Vicky could not do. If she were ever inclined to forget her self-styled role as her parents' ambassador, the letters which daily arrived from home would have reminded her that she was first and foremost Princess Royal of England.

The Hohenzollerns, already suspicious of the innovation of an English marriage, were not won over by finding in their midst a young woman who was openly critical of their 'busy idleness', and preferred lectures on chemistry to family gossip. She found fault with the uncomfortable schlosses, the primitive plumbing, the lack of cultural facilities in Berlin, the backward place of women in Prussian society, proclaiming how much better things were organised in England.

At the end of the year, a doctor and nurse were sent out from England for Vicky's first confinement. On 27 January 1859 a son was born who was later to be known as 'Kaiser Bill'. 'May he', wrote his English grandmother, 'be a blessing and comfort to you and to his country.' The birth had been a protracted and diffi-cult one, and once the baby had been safely born, the doctors' first care was for the exhausted mother. It was not until the baby was three days old that it was discovered his left shoulder and arm had been so badly wrenched that the arm was dangling useless. At first the injury seemed quickly curable and hardly shadowed Vicky's pride and delight in her son, but soon 'Willy' was having his good arm strapped to his side for an hour a day – the first in a

Queen Victoria with her grandson Wilhelm of Prussia

long series of hopeless efforts to bring the maimed arm into use.

In 1861 Fritz's father, the Prince of Prussia, succeeded his brother to the throne as King Wilhelm I. He shocked enlightened British opinion by crowning himself with the significant words '. . . this crown comes to me from God alone'. The King had not listened to Albert's advice; he intended to rule despotically,

Wilhelm I of Prussia

backed by a strengthened army. He was already sixty-four, courteous, simple, conservative and honourable, a tall, stiff man with a wide-boned face and formidable side whiskers; a soldier by training and inclination, he slept under an army blanket on a camp-bed. Comparisons with Franz Josef are tempting, but soon falter: Wilhelm I was none too bright, and his ambition never more than to preserve the *status quo* in his native state. The first Hohenzollern to become King of Prussia had been crowned at Königsburg in 1701, and that was good enough for Wilhelm. His concept of social structure was elementary: 'It is for the army to defend the crown, and Prussia's kings have never known the army waver in its loyalty.'

Two years later, a serious clash arose between king and parliament over the question of increased army estimates. Rather than give in, Wilhelm offered to abdicate in favour of his son, now Crown Prince. Fritz, in whose gentle and honourable nature hesitation was a flaw, hesitated fatally. The King withdrew his offer, and instead sent for Bismarck. Within a few days he had been appointed Minister President with enormous powers.

Perhaps the best thumb-nail portrait of Bismarck is a recent one:

At first glance, Bismarck seemed a typical representative of the class from which he sprang – the Junkers. He was tall, bull-necked, bulbous-eyed, florid-faced and energetic, with a hearty appetite, great physical stamina and a tremendous zest for life. He had a deep love of the countryside, of forests, farms and wild animals and was never happier, it seemed, than when out walking under the trees with his dogs. He might have been no more than a successful country squire. But, on closer acquaintance, it all looked a little too good to be true. . . . Bismarck's was a many-faceted personality. He was an intelligent, cultivated, well-spoken man of the world, witty and cynical. He could be utterly charming. Yet, for all his urbanity, he was an emotional man, with a restless manner, a high-pitched voice and eyes likely to spill over with tears. He had a violent temper. Extremely sensitive, he neither forgot nor forgave an insult. He was astute, devious, perceptive; also dynamic, ambitious and ruthless. His heart could be like stone. Above all, Bismarck had a lust for power.[1]

This mountain of paradoxes towered over Europe for almost thirty years. Nearly twenty years younger than the King, he had already served as Prussian Minister to the Diet of the German Confederation at Frankfurt – where he challenged the paramountcy of the Austrians with studied and outrageous insolence – and as Ambassador to St Petersburg, where he met the Tsar, and to Paris, where he met Napoleon III. His extreme and chauvinistic conservatism, which had kept him out of office, now swept him in. The moral precepts of Prince Albert and King Leopold failed to impress him – he dismissed them as 'Anglo–Coburg heresies'. He was, above all, a skilled technician in *realpolitik,* for which he found a divine excuse: 'I am content when I can see where the Lord wishes me to go, and can stumble after him'.

His horizons were continental: nothing beyond Europe interested him, everything inside it did. Coming from East Prussia, his greatest fear was of an attack by Russia, the traditional enemy of the Teutonic Knights; he cultivated his friendship with the Romanovs and shaped his foreign policy to placate and neutralise them. He was a late convert to the policy of

Otto von Bismarck with his wife

unifying Germany, and had no intention of creating it as a constitutional democracy: the path the Lord pointed out to him led to a Germany united by Prussian military strength, and progress along it needed to be cautious, to avoid antagonising greater powers.

His attitude to the role of the state was an expansion of the King's, and the two of them got along well enough, in a knockabout sort of way. 'His Majesty is like a horse. He takes fright at any unaccustomed object and grows obstinate if driven, but gradually gets used to it,' Bismarck said, and prevailed at moments of crisis by smashing the royal china and joining his master in torrential weeping. Wilhelm complained that it was a hard thing to rule under Bismarck, but he followed where the Mad Junker led.

Prussia was a small country, and Berlin an ugly, unfashionable city in the middle of a dark, northern plain; within a few years it was to be the political centre of Europe. Bismarck's immediate objectives were to enforce the power of the monarchy and to strengthen the Prussian army. He dissolved parliament, spent the taxes without their approval, and proclaimed his famous thesis that 'the great questions of the day aren't decided by speeches and resolutions of majorities, but by iron and blood'. He was not without opponents. There have always been two Germanys: one the home of philosophy, romantic sensibility and altruistic high-mindedness; the other the fatherland of disciplined followers of despotic leadership. In the 1860s there was still doubt as to which of these two forces within the German *zeit* was to prevail; but in this schizophrenic battle Bismarck was a formidable leader. To his opponents he showed a ruthlessness which even followed them beyond the grave. The Crown Prince was one of them.

At the end of 1861 Albert Prince Consort died, worn out by overwork and noble despair, and Vicky found herself suddenly cut off from the help and counsel without which she could not imagine directing her life in an alien country. Like her mother, she pledged herself emotionally to continue his policies, to be guided only by what *he* would have thought right. 'I am but beginning life and the unerring judgment on which I built with so much security and so much confidence is gone!' she confessed to Victoria. 'I am only twenty-one and things here wear a threatening aspect.'

The funeral cortège of Prince Albert

Queen Victoria in 1862

Vicky with her children Wilhelm and Charlotte

In 1863 she persuaded Fritz to give encouragement to the liberal faction by disassociating himself – first in a letter and then openly in a speech – from his father's and Bismarck's recent restriction on the freedom of the press. 'Your beloved Papa', the Queen assured her, 'looks down and approves.' The King's furious reaction distressed Fritz, a devoted son, but he remained firm. Vicky relished the drama of the conflict, and declared herself 'prepared for catastrophe!' But there was no catastrophic outcome. Bismarck would not risk making a popular martyr. He urged the King to 'deal gently with the young man Absalom'. Fritz was grudgingly forgiven on the promise that he would keep silent on political matters in future. From then onwards the only

Fritz

encouragement he felt able to give the Liberal cause was the negative one of taking no part in the political affairs of the country. It was hard for him, harder still for his ambitious wife, to fade into political obscurity; but King Wilhelm, in his sixties, was ageing visibly. They did not expect to have to wait very long.

During the following years, the Crown Prince was entirely excluded from political affairs. He remained, however, a popular figure of patent sincerity and splendid golden-bearded looks. No such affection was accorded his wife. She considered herself 'as good a patriot as any of them', but she was intolerant and tactless, and her influence over her husband was well known and distrusted. 'They consider me', she said, 'la génie du mal.' Their

Fritz with Willy in about 1865

enmity with Bismarck continued. His spies infiltrated their
entourage. The Crown Prince sometimes found himself in agreement with 'the great man', but between the Princess and Bismarck
there was implacable dislike. To him, she was 'Die Engländerin';
and she – in other fields so quick to respond to new ideas – held
rigidly to the precepts laid down by the Prince Consort, and
hated every step of Bismarck's policy.

Through all their trials the marriage prospered. Vicky considered Fritz her 'golden lot', and he depended more and more
on his 'frauchen'. Their friends were drawn from the fields of
arts and science, and visitors found their household delightful

Vicky with Willy

and stimulating. Their family increased steadily, eight children in all being born. Vicky was a conscientious mother and adored babies, but with older children was inclined, she admitted, to 'play the policeman'. Her standards were high, and Willy the chief cause of her concern: he was a lively, affectionate, attractive child; but she soon noticed that he flew into a passion 'when he does not want to do a thing'. This trait was worsened by the frustrations of his useless arm – he could neither feed nor dress himself – and the various attempted cures which he had to endure. He did exercises with an army sergeant, was clamped into a machine to strengthen his neck, and was even given – at his mother's insistence – the new electric treatment. The arm, however, remained foreshortened and useless. At last it was decided that, as improvement was not possible, Willy must learn to manage as though he had two good arms. This meant further anguish. He was taught to find his balance on horseback by riding without stirrups, his tutor forcing the frightened child on to the pony's back each time he was thrown. The future ruler of Prussia had to be able to ride well.

His mother prided herself on watching over 'every detail, even the minutest', of his education. She felt there was a deep bond between them. Sadly, in retrospect, he saw her as 'exacting and remote'. He felt more of a bond with his English grandmother. Visits to Windsor and Osborne, where he shared the nursery with his young uncles and aunts, laid the foundations of the love-hate relationship with England which lasted all his life. He was a great favourite with Queen Victoria, but she was lovingly aware of his faults, especially that streak of arrogance in his nature which showed itself early. She urged his mother to 'bring him up simply' and let him mix more freely with ordinary people. Soldiers, she thought, were not good company for him: 'They are not free.'

But soldiering was Willy's great interest, and one which his Prussian grandfather encouraged. King Wilhelm made much of the boy and delighted in encouraging what Queen Victoria called 'that dreadful Prussian pride and ambition which grieved Papa so much'. Prussia, in fact, was booming, and Bismarck feeling his way towards relieving Austria of the leadership of Germany. The Holy Roman Empire, from which Franz Josef claimed his inheritance, had long ago bequeathed to Austria the status of first nation in German Europe, and the Austrians still dominated the Confederation of North German states. Bismarck decided it was time they went. He was more aware than most of the beleaguered and isolated state of Franz Josef's empire; but he needed a plausible excuse to challenge it. The excuse came in the unlikely guise of a dynastic crisis in Schleswig Holstein.

Lord Palmerston is reputed to have said, 'Only three men have ever understood it. One was Prince Albert, who is dead. The second was a German professor who went mad. I am the third and I have forgotten all about it.' Out of this tortuous and unmemorable affair, Bismarck managed to pick a quarrel with Austria. He made a quick arrangement with Napoleon which assured French neutrality and a simultaneous Italian attack on the Austrians in Venetia, and mobilised the Prussian army.

Bismarck was no lover of war. 'It's a clumsy method,' he said, 'but one tries every way – the most dangerous last. . . . No one who has seen men dying on the battlefield would lightly fight.' With humanity on the side of expediency, he and the leader of the Prussian Army, von Moltke, struck fast and without warning, using the latest invention in quick-firing armament – the needle gun. In the modern European sense of the term, it was the first *blitzkrieg*.

On 15 June 1866 Prussian troops crossed the frontiers of Hanover, Saxony and Hesse, one army marching through Hanover to the River Main which, roughly speaking, divides North from South Germany. After several smaller battles had forced the Austrians into retreat, the two armies faced each other at Königgratz, known as Sadowa, in Austria. The two Prussian forces which attacked the Austrian line were joined, when the battle was in the balance, by a third, commanded by the Crown Prince, and it was quickly over. The Austrian army was decimated, losing over 44,000 men. Another horrifying defeat was added to Magenta and Solferino.

The Crown Prince, for all his liberalism, had been brought up in the military traditions of the Hohenzollerns, and was no mean soldier. Nor was he averse to a move to unify North Germany under Prussia. He accepted command of the Prussian Second Army with pride and misgiving, and had already won other victories before Sadowa. Vicky was less enthusiastic. 'For me,' she said, 'this war will ever be a crime, brought on by the irresponsibility and temerity of one man.' But she was torn. 'What do you say to all these dreadful battles?' she asked her mother. 'Are you not a little pleased that it is our Fritz alone who has won all these victories?' Victoria thought little of them: Hanover

Battle of Sadowa. The Crown Prince's army advances.

was her ancestral home, and the spectacle of independent German states being overrun by Junkers did not appeal at all to her. As Vicky remarked, 'What would dearest Papa say to all this? He would be shocked and distressed beyond measure.'

Bismarck had broken Austria's centuries-old influence over North Germany in ten days, and swept all the little states north of the Main into an alliance under Prussia. He was anxious to call it a day before other powers, particularly Russia, became restive; nor did he desire the break-up of Franz Josef's empire, which he saw as a future ally against Russian pressure from the east; in addition, a magnanimous peace would add to Prussia's prestige.

The King thought otherwise. He had been reluctant to cross his borders, but once he had smelt gunpowder he was eager to charge on to Vienna. Bismarck argued with him, broke a doorknob, and threatened to throw himself out of a window. In the end, Fritz persuaded his father to take his triumphant armies home. The curiously assorted conquerors withdrew. The Prussians had made their first short march towards German unity, and there was something a little sinister about their gait.

Chapter three

Our Beautiful Providence

In the summer nights of 1866, the Prussian campfires could be seen from Vienna. The Empress Elizabeth and her children were sent off to Hungary, for the city was no longer defensible. For ten years Franz Josef had personally led a maniacal outburst of demolition and rebuilding in his capital: the medieval walls had been torn down and a huge circular avenue, the *Ringstrasse*, laid in their place; whole districts had been flattened for the building of a hundred new streets and squares and for five hundred great civic buildings, including a new Opera House. Strauss had written a 'Demolition Polka'; a bubble of business speculation rose above the city; the meadows beyond the old walls were landscaped into gardens and parks; and in the centre of it the Imperial Palace of Schönbrunn lay like a vast rococo jewel in its new setting. There Franz Josef sat and worked in his private apartments, which he and Sisi had refurnished with large, regrettable pieces from Tottenham Court Road.

After the defeat at Sadowa the hospitals overflowed and an urgent sense of doom pervaded the city. The Austrians, after all, were Germans themselves, suddenly cut off from their own kind. One of them – Grillparzer, the poet – informed the Prussians, 'You believe you have given birth to an empire, but you have only destroyed a people.' Franz Josef, miserably alone, signed away North Germany to Prussia, paid a large indemnity, ceded Venetia to the Italians, and prayed to be left in peace; but he reckoned without the Hungarians.

Elizabeth arrived in Budapest uncertain of her welcome. Kossuth, from exile, was raising revolutionary Hungarian levies to help the Prussians, and the old Magyar hopes of independence were rekindling. 'One more Austrian reverse,' it was reported in Budapest, 'and a rising is certain.' In the event, she was received with rapture and the Hungarian leader Deák announced, 'I should have considered it an act of cowardice to turn my back on the Empress in the day of her misfortune, after we had done homage to her when all was going well with the dynasty.' He assured the Emperor that his country would ask 'nothing more after Sadowa than before it'. These assurances, however, were not entirely disinterested. Franz Josef's position was in some ways strengthened by defeat. No individual country within the Hapsburg lands was capable of withstanding, by itself, an enemy from outside them. Russia or Prussia could easily pick them off singly if the collective strength of the Empire were destroyed, and recent events had shown this to be possible. Imperial rule might be a scourge, but it was also a shield, and few of Franz Josef's subjects wanted that shield to disintegrate.

Franz Josef still owned all the Danube lands, and a great deal of South-east Europe down to the Balkans. His own inclination was towards some kind of federal administration, centred in Vienna, in which all national and racial components – German, Magyar or Slavic – would be represented. The Hungarians wanted no part of this: their claim had always been equality with Austria as an independent Magyar nation under the crown, regardless of what happened to the rest. 'You look after your Slavs,' Andrassy told the Emperor, 'and we will look after ours.' It is easy to exaggerate Elizabeth's part in the deadlock and *détente* which followed; but she was an influence, and they in turn influenced her to an extent which affected the fate of the Hapsburg family.

Ferenc Deák was a quiet, pipe-smoking Hungarian lawyer of great intellect and honesty, unambitious and incorruptible. He had served in the revolutionary Ministry of 1848 and been court-martialled and acquitted in 1849; for the rest of his life he moved with the greatest caution. Unlike Kossuth, he recognised that Hungary could only survive in association with Austria – 'We must admit,' he said, 'that by ourselves we are not a great

Franz Josef in 1862

Ferenc Deák

Julius Andrassy

state' – and he slowly built up a movement in Budapest which demanded only a reasonable, constitutional form of internal self-government in return for loyalty to the Emperor of Austria as King of Hungary: the old idea of Dual Monarchy. Franz Josef found this unacceptable, but Elizabeth did not.

Since her visit in 1857 Elizabeth had learnt Hungarian, and now spoke it well. Her mother-in-law's dislike of the country inclined her towards it. She replaced many of her Austrian entourage with Hungarians – an act of patronage which dimmed her popularity in Vienna – and began to study Hungarian history and politics in earnest. The seeds sown by Count Majlath in her girlhood had grown and now flowered. In 1866 she met Count Andrassy and was enchanted by him.

Since his return from exile, Andrassy had worked as an ardent and active nationalist with Deák, whose exact opposite he was: ambitious, bold, witty and 'a far more interesting person in appearance . . . in Hungarian dress, with the black locks and handsome face of a romantic bandit'.[1] He was equally captivated by the Empress; but he was one of the few men who did not give in to her whims, and she respected him all her life.

While Franz Josef worked alone in Vienna, among the ugly English furniture, Andrassy and Elizabeth lived as much as possible in each other's company in Budapest. They talked and

Empress Elizabeth

rode together, made clandestine expeditions to country fairs – which must have reminded her of her childhood with her father – and tasted together such delights of Magyar life as she had always imagined. He was possibly in love with her, possibly her lover – Valerie, her youngest and favourite child, born in Budapest in 1868, was said to be his – but he was a patriot and politician above all, and determined to use her influence with the Emperor. In July he noted in his diary, 'If we are successful, Hungary owes more than she guesses to the beautiful Providence watching over her.'

Elizabeth began to write to Franz Josef a stream of letters begging him to reach a settlement with Hungary and to make Andrassy his chief Hungarian Minister and even Imperial Minister for Foreign Affairs. The Emperor demurred: 'The Hungarian Constitution must be solved with reference to the rest of the Monarchy.' Elizabeth insisted, and resorted to emotional blackmail; long after the Prussian danger was past, she stayed in Budapest, refusing to come home.

Through their separation, Franz Josef remained as deeply and hopelessly in love with her as ever; but he also remained adamant. He wrote:

My dear Sisi, my best thanks for your letter – the whole of which has only one purpose, to demonstrate to me with a whole assortment of reasons that you want to stay in Ofen with the children, and will. Since you must know that I cannot go from here, [and] that it would go clean against my duty to adopt your exclusively Hungarian standpoint, neglecting those other lands which have borne immense suffering with steadfast loyalty and at this particular moment deserve particular attention and care, you will understand that I cannot visit you. If you find the air here unhealthy, so be it – and I shall have to console myself as best I may and patiently put up with my long-accustomed loneliness.

Gradually, they wore him down. In February 1867 a compromise was reached between Austria and Hungary – the *Ausgleich*. Elizabeth returned to Vienna, and she and Franz Josef were reconciled. The Viennese were less forgiving. In all likelihood some solution along the lines of the Dual Monarchy would have been reached eventually without her, but the legend that it was her doing took root. From now on Franz Josef held the title of His Apostolic Majesty the King-Emperor of Austria-Hungary, and in June of that year he and Elizabeth went together in state to be crowned King and Queen of Hungary. Andrassy was created Minister for Hungary. The Slavs and others who 'deserve particular attention and care' were left to shift for themselves.

1867 was the year of the Great Exhibition in Paris. Napoleon III was feeling an acute need for prestige and friendship, not least for friendship with Austria-Hungary. Italy no longer needed him. His most extravagant adventure – the creation of a new Mexican Empire, with Franz Josef's brother Maximilian as emperor – was foundering. Prussia was creating a strong and aggressive Germany across the Rhine. When he suggested to the Austrian government that the time had come for a military pact, with Italy and against Prussia, he found the Austrians disinclined to make common cause against the invader who had recently

The coronation of Franz Josef as King of Hungary, 1867

spared them. 'What our monarchy wants', he was told, 'is the maintenance of peace.' France was now alone.

On the other hand, with the fading importance of Vienna Paris had become the cultural centre of Western Europe, and the achievements of Napoleon's own reign seemed substantial enough to warrant celebration. With memories of Prince Albert's Crystal Palace triumph in mind, Napoleon felt that it was his turn to put on a show which would make friends and influence people.

Paris in the 1860s was not only the centre of culture but the centre of fun, and the Great Exhibition was the greatest fun of all. Workmen, entertainers and whores came from all over France; the *Champ du Mars* was transformed into a stately pleasure-dome in which the nations of the world displayed their wares, and outside the official orbit opera and ballet flourished and fashion became outrageous; the enormous concourse of visitors was regaled with the music of Offenbach, and Strauss – never one to miss an occasion – contributed a new waltz, *The Blue Danube*.

That taint of enthusiastic amateurism, which infected the whole of Napoleon's reign, hung ominously about the *Champ du Mars,* which was deep in mud and disorder on the eve of opening, but the weather and chaos cleared and the crowned heads and their emissaries rolled in: from England the Prince of Wales (who enjoyed it immensely), from Russia Tsar Alexander II, from further afield the Sultan of Turkey, the Pasha of Egypt, and a clutter of minor royalty. The affair was an enormous social success. The exhibition itself gave a little more cause of reflec-

Napoleon III

tion; it included French art, British locomotives, a new American invention called the rocking-chair, and, from Prussia, the biggest piece of armament in the world, a black, 50-ton Krupp gun, made to fire 1000-lb. shells.

Franz Josef and Sisi were expected to arrive after their coronation in Hungary, although Elizabeth disliked the French Empress Eugénie, whom she considered common; but in the third week of June news came from Mexico that the Emperor Maximilian, abandoned by Napoleon in the face of the Monroe Doctrine, had been overthrown and shot. They cancelled their visit.

It was not the occasion's only diplomatic failure. By far the French Emperor's biggest catch was the Tsar of all the Russias, that huge, unknowable territory which had eluded even Napoleon I. If he could be made the partner of an entente, then Germany would be contained. Alexander was reluctant to come to Paris, having some reason to fear assassination; but he did arrive, and was immediately shot at by a young Polish anarchist, who missed and was taken into custody. Unhurt but very angry, Alexander threatened to leave at once and was only persuaded to stay by Napoleon's promise of a review of 40,000 French troops.

A performance in the Chinese theatre at the Paris Exhibition

Somehow, only 20,000 turned up, and something went wrong with the charge. The Tsar returned to St Petersburg with the strong conviction that the Second French Empire was not an ally he needed.

The Prussians also paid a visit: King Wilhelm, Fritz, Bismarck, and some army officers who made a quiet reconnaissance of the Paris fortifications. The King behaved very properly, and when consulted by Napoleon about precedence said that the Tsar must go before him, being an emperor. Fritz, normally mild, was stung by the inferiority of mere kingship. 'That', he announced, 'no Hohenzollern is ever to say again.'

As summer ended, the captains and kings departed, leaves fell and the exhibition frayed sadly at the edges. The party, for Napoleon, was nearly over, but he made one more attempt to attract the Apostolic King-Emperor of Austria-Hungary. Franz Josef – moved by duty and a deep sense of protocol – went eventually to Paris. Elizabeth, once more preoccupied by her own interests, failed to accompany him.

In many ways Franz Josef was no fool. He had taken the hint that the Prussians wanted no more quarrelling between Germans, and he trusted Bismarck more than Napoleon – a shrewd enough choice of evils. He rather enjoyed the exhibition, but nothing important was agreed between him and the French Emperor. All the same, he completed Napoleon's royal flush. That summer all the great crowned heads of Europe were gathered together in one place, and over them loomed the big, black Krupp gun.

Chapter four

A Change of Empires

When Fritz returned from the Austrian war, Vicky passionately upbraided him for falling into step with Bismarck. Fritz promised 'not to be led astray again', but the temptations were great. The Austrian campaign had made it clear that Prussia was the first power in a divided land, but it would take a greater crisis to stampede the small independent states into accepting the King of Prussia as their emperor, and this Bismarck was about to supply.

Bismarck had stumped after the army to Sadowa, in the uniform of a major in the reserve, and came back as a Count, with the King more deeply indebted to him than ever. 'He is a most unprincipled and unrespectable character,' Vicky complained, 'but the king is determined to uphold him.' Bismarck had little regard for outward show, so long as no one was preferred to himself. He once said, 'His Majesty has given me the Order of the Grand Cross. I'd rather have had a horse or a barrel of good Rheinish wine.' He drank a great deal, and ate more, and waited for events to play into his hands: 'The river of history flows as it will, and if I put my hand in it, it is because I regard it as my duty, not because I think I can change its course. Man cannot create the current of events. He can only float with it and steer.' When the moment came, he could steer with enormous force and skill. Meanwhile he returned to his estate to enjoy life among his family and trees; but every day the dispatch boxes reached him from Berlin, and he worked at them in the night, a choleric

Bismarck

giant, with red hair turning grey, in a silent country house.

What Napoleon most hoped for – the squeezing of Prussia between Russia in the East and France in the West – was what Bismarck most feared. By dealing with Austria, he had secured his southern flank; what he needed was a pretext for giving France a similar knock, in the course of which he could pull Germany together under single rule. One came three years after the Paris Exhibition, in 1870.

It was the flimsiest of things. In Madrid a dissolute and legally childless queen, Isabella II, was pushed off the Spanish throne, and Bismarck backed a young Hohenzollern prince to take her place. Apart from the Bonapartes, nineteenth-century royalty was very much a closed shop, and a vacant crown generally accepted as a perk for one of the boys. Predictably, Napoleon objected to having a second Prussian-led kingdom to his south, and demanded that the Hohenzollerns withdraw their candidate and promise never to propose another. Pride, on both sides, was at risk.

To understand the Ems telegram incident which followed, it is

Fritz

necessary to appreciate the almost childlike innocence of King Wilhelm. He was in the habit of going to the spa at Ems to take the waters, and dressed and behaved there like any modest, respectable elderly gentleman. It is said that once, taking his afternoon constitutional with his friend Count Lehndorff, he saw Bismarck, with whom he had quarrelled that morning, approaching and was panic-stricken. 'Can't we get into a side-street?' he asked Lehndorff. 'He's so upset he'll cut me.' In the end, he and Bismarck went off together to chat on a bench over-looking the river.

In July 1870 Wilhelm was at Ems without Bismarck, when the French Ambassador brought him the demand from Paris. They too sat on a bench and discussed possible ways of defusing a situation which had inflamed French public opinion against Prussia and Prussian opinion equally against France. After Sadowa Wilhelm had said publicly that he hoped he would be allowed to reign within the new Confederation in peace and quiet, and he meant it. He drafted a long, conciliatory telegram to Napoleon, acceding to the first half of his request while politely rejecting the other. Painstakingly correct, he sent the draft to Bismarck to dispatch.

Bismarck was in Berlin, waiting for the French to take the unforgivable first step. The Prussian army was ready; Von Moltke had told him: 'We have only to press a button'. Finding Wilhelm's draft insufficiently provocative, Bismarck edited it, and sent it to Paris in the King's name. It took only a few minutes to light this fuse. The French exploded in an agony of outraged *amour propre,* and declared war. In the eyes of the world, Prussia was once again the victim of Napoleonic aggression.

Even Vicky was taken in, and appealed to England for help in 'a war we are forced into against our will'. But Britain remained neutral, and so did the rest of Europe. The French Grand Army was probably still invincible. Everybody held their breath. Fritz put on his uniform and took command of a force from Württemburg and Bavaria, and the combined German armies stood to as the French troops approached. On 4 August von Moltke took the initiative and invaded France.

Any doubts as to which side had the superior fighting force were soon resolved. 'Although the French fought with great *élan,* they were no match for the superbly organised Prussians.'[1] That lack of solid professionalism which characterised Napoleon III's régime encompassed its end; his soldiers were brave, many and determined to defend their own country, but the machinery behind them was shoddy and they could do little to stop the progress of the Prussian-led German forces towards Metz. At the beginning of September Napoleon and his main army were beaten, encircled and forced to surrender at Sedan. It was an even greater military achievement than Sadowa: in three days the French lost nearly 100,000 men and their Emperor.

Bismarck would have been happy to call it a day, and to treat France as he had treated Austria: his intention had been to establish Prussia in a position of power and security in the centre of Europe, and he feared a war of attrition, in the short term because of the danger of Austrian, Russian, or British intervention, and in the long term because a completely defeated and humiliated France would be – and in fact was – a dangerously resentful neighbour for at least a generation. He had no territorial ambitions – 'We do not want any disgruntled Frenchmen in Germany,' he said. 'Let each tribe stay in its own lands.' But

Prussian troops attacking at the battle of Sedan

this time he could not hold back the generals who, for strategic reasons, insisted on Alsace, Lorraine and the fortress of Metz as the price of peace. The French, bereft of their Emperor, formed a republican government and scraped up fresh troops, and the war continued. Not for the last time, the German army, with its steel-grey paraphernalia, lumbered across Northern France towards Paris.

Fritz's army had fought well and he was rewarded by the Iron Cross and the Max Josef medal of Bavaria, but as the war went deeper into France his enthusiasm for it evaporated. 'It is strange that I, who would rather gain recognition by works of peace, should win such blood-stained laurels,' he wrote in his diary.

Bismarck had less scruple. To his mind the achievement of an early peace justified the most violent means, and with his approval open towns were shelled and prisoners of war shot in an attempt to break the remaining resistance. 'I am appalled,' the Crown Prince wrote, 'by the behaviour of our soldiers, and the ruthlessness of our command – particularly Bismarck. He has made us great and powerful, but he has robbed us of our friends, of the sympathy of the world, and of our conscience.'

Matters between Fritz and Bismarck came to a head when the German High Command reached Versailles. The Crown Prince was placed in charge of the German forces investing Paris. In October the French surrendered Metz with over 170,000 men, and their new government withdrew to Tours, leaving the capital as their only bastion against the enemy. Fritz and his colleagues in the German High Command believed that Paris could be reduced by siege. He had no love of that 'modern Babylon', but considered that bombardment would be wasteful of human lives and uncertain of success: 'I felt a lump rise in my throat as I thought of the innocent folk who have to suffer – above all, the children who may possibly be hit.' But the Parisians faced starvation with surprising fortitude.

Lord Gower, who visited the besieged city, reported 'terrible sufferings in the poorer quarters where houses were pulled down without rhyme or reason, the bricks being used for ineffectual barricades, while the homeless families sat in the streets clutching their miserable possessions, exposed to the wind and to the rain which poured down without mercy that autumn. It was said that cats, dogs and even rats were eaten for food. There was dysentery and sickness without end.'[2] As weeks turned to months without capitulation, Bismarck insisted with growing violence that Paris be shelled. Fritz refused. He was supported in

The Crown Prince, Commander-in-Chief of the Southern Army, with his General staff at their headquarters, Les Ombrayes, 13 January 1871

this by Vicky, and it did not improve their standing either with Bismarck or in Berlin. Vicky, who had embarked on a crusade of military hospital improvement, was working among the wounded at Hamburg. She was sent back to Berlin by the King and publicly (though not formally) accused of frustrating the German war effort.

The King himself was at Versailles, a confused and irascible old man who tried to set an example by eating dry bread, and mediated uncertainly between the generals and Bismarck. The dimensions of the future were palpably beyond him; from time to time he threatened to abdicate in favour of Fritz, but always relapsed into a grumbling acceptance of his duty. Versailles became a hot-house of quarrel and intrigue, of boredom and strain, and of the combined tensions of court and army. It was a scene of baroque fantasy. While Bismarck negotiated over champagne and food sent from his estates, Fritz ate bread with his father and went off to *le roi soleil's* chapel to sing to the organ.

Apart from reducing Paris, the Germans' main concern was for the unity of their nation. The patriotism of war had already predisposed the peoples and parliaments of the individual states to unite under the kingship of Prussia, but the princes were less inclined to give up their rights and Wilhelm would accept an

imperial crown only from them. In fact, he was reluctant to consider it at all, and to receive it from elected parliaments involved the recognition of a constitutional government which neither he nor Bismarck was prepared to entertain. Why, he asked, should he exchange 'the splendid crown of Prussia for a crown of filth'?

The Crown Prince had no such reservations; a united Germany was what he and his faction had always wanted, and he hoped soon to have the privilege of reigning over it in a constitutional manner: 'On me and mine devolves the task of setting our hands in true German fashion to build the mighty edifice on principles in conformity with modern times and free from prejudice.' Bismarck accused him of suffering from 'Emperormadness'. While booted men from Potsdam marched across the delicate floors of the most famous palace of the world, the three leaders were locked in combat, Bismarck wanting an autocratic empire, Fritz a constitutional one, and Wilhelm to be left alone.

As usual, Bismarck prevailed. He invited the German princes to Versailles, where they made a bizarre addition to the motley company in occupation. The rulers of Baden, Hesse and Württemburg proved reasonably tractable, but Ludwig II of Bavaria – the 'mad king', first cousin to Elizabeth of Austria – was too wild and woolly-headed to be brought to heel. In desperation Bismarck bribed him to offer the crown to Wilhelm, on behalf of all his peers, in return for an income of £15,000 a year with which to build follies, and the deed was done. On 18 January 1871, after tears, tantrums, prayers and desultory breaking of crockery, Wilhelm was crowned in Louis XIV's Hall of Mirrors as German Emperor – a title of compromise which he did not appreciate – and tottered from the platform in an Imperial huff while a German band played the *Hohenfriedburg* march.

Earlier in the month, Fritz had been prevailed upon to shell the outer defences of Paris, and the city surrendered on 28 January, one day after the French government had signed a humiliating armistice and dissolved itself pending a general election. On 1 March the Prussian leaders held a military parade in the city, and were greeted by empty streets and blackveiled monuments; it was a glum contrast to their visit three years earlier with all the fireworks and Offenbach.

The German troops withdrew, and months later held another parade in the more sympathetic atmosphere of Berlin. The newly

Ludwig II of Bavaria   *Wilhelm I*

The proclamation of Wilhelm I as Emperor of Germany at Versailles 18 January 1871

Adolphe Thiers

created Kaiser rode in triumph at the head of his forces with Fritz, and Willy – aged twelve – on a dappled pony. 'Never shall I forget that day,' Willy wrote later. 'I myself rode behind my father on to the Unter den Linden, where a huge red and gold canopy was supported on four gilt columns, and on each of the columns was a figure of Victory!'

Wilhelm treated Napoleon with some courtesy. He provided him with a country house near Fresnes until the war was over, and then allowed him to travel to England to join the Empress Eugénie, who had been smuggled out of Paris by an American dentist. Those who remained in their ex-capital were less fortunate.

When news of the armistice reached Paris there were riots, and although a new and conservative French Republican government was formed in February, it settled itself at Versailles, along with the Germans, rather than risk entering the city. The head of this government was Adolphe Thiers, a man of seventy-three but still a dominating intelligence and a brilliant opportunist politician of the old school, the last surviving pupil of Talley-rand. He was a brisk little man with twinkling spectacles and an enormous head, fluent, sarcastic, persuasive, emotional and vain; highly gifted, extremely competent. His aim was to restore order, stability, prosperity and pride to France, at the price of buying off the Germans, and he was already on good terms with Bismarck, who had considerable respect and affection for Thiers – one day before leaving Versailles, finding the old man asleep, he wrapped his own cloak around him. Bismarck also offered some advice about Paris: 'Provoke the insurrection while you still have the power, in order that you may crush it for good' – and promised what help he could, although officially Germany was no longer involved.

The defence of Paris during the siege had been taken over by a citizens' militia – the National Guard – when the government left, and by the beginning of March 1871 their leaders had formed a Central Committee to administer the city. The mass of Parisians were already suspicious of France's new bourgeois government and the old antagonisms of the June Days of 1848 revived when, on 18 March, Thiers sent government troops to the city with orders to disarm the National Guard. Thiers' soldiers were thrown out, and from then on an undeclared state of war existed between Paris and the Versailles government.

On 26 March the Central Committee in Paris stepped down to make way for a Commune, which was voted into being by a general election in the city two days later. Apart from some liberals, who soon resigned, the Commune comprised a majority of Jacobins who looked back to the old French revolutionary traditions, and a minority of socialists who looked forward to new prospects suggested by Karl Marx. But although their immediate aims soon merged, in their desperate defence of the city, the main force within the Paris Commune was not inter-national communism but a patriotic revolutionist fervour inherited from the past.

Outstanding among the veteran revolutionists was Delescluze, an old man who had fought at the barricades in 1830 and 1848. His health had been broken by years of penal servitude, but he was indomitable. Throughout the life of the Commune he wore

Paris 1871. Troops of the Commune in front of the column in Place Vendôme, and, below, the Place after the column had been toppled.

A balloon leaving besieged Paris in 1871

the uniform of 1848 – top hat, frock coat, black trousers and a red sash around his waist. Some of the younger, more truly socialist Communards were women, notably Louise Michel, an anarchist schoolteacher who led the Central Committee of the Union of Women. Like all the rest, they were pledged to a doomed cause.

At first the Commune governed Paris undisturbed, receiving food supplies from the north, where the Prussians were still in occupation and formally neutral; but Thiers – with Bismarck's permission – was bringing together an army of 150,000, supported by some two hundred heavy guns, to face the 100,000 National Guards who defended the capital. Thiers' army attacked the outer defences on 2 April and by 10 May had fought its way close to the city walls. On 23 May government troops managed to infiltrate the city and street-fighting began.

Prisoners were shot, and hostages taken by both sides, yet the determination of the garrison grew as its situation became more desperate. Day after day, street after street, Paris was defended, with enormous losses. When all was lost, Delescluze, still in his

62 hostages are executed by the Communards during the Civil War between the new French government and the Paris Commune

1848 uniform, said goodbye to his comrades, and walked quietly down an enfiladed street. He climbed the barricade at the end and stood there a moment, then fell forward, shot dead.

Hundreds of Parisians were subsequently executed by the government (in all 20,000 died in the course of the rebellion) and another 20,000 were deported or imprisoned, but the spirit of revolt was not quite killed. Louise Michel, for one, wrote from her prison cell, 'If you let me live, I shall not cease calling for vengeance. If you are not cowards, kill me.' They did not kill her but sent her to New Caledonia, from where she returned later to become a leading anarchist.

Paris was gutted and the focus of European affairs moved to Berlin; the French Empire was ended and the German Empire born; and in those few months of 1871 a new revolutionary inspiration was also born, which was to outlive every empire.

German troops on the Place de la Concorde in Paris in 1871

Chapter five
The Three Kaisers

The new German constitution turned out to be remarkably like the old Prussian one: Wilhelm was supported by a Council of Ministers with whom he was not obliged to agree, and Bismarck, as Chancellor, by a parliament – the *Reichstag* – which he could manipulate at will. The outburst at Paris had sent a shudder through the courts of Europe and confirmed Bismarck in his conservatism: it was hardly a time for liberal reform.

It is hard to tell whether Bismarck genuinely feared revolution or merely used the spectre of it to scare the Romanovs and Hapsburgs into the arms of the Hohenzollerns; but he quickly persuaded Wilhelm, Franz Josef and the Tsar to stand together against anarchy and republicanism and so, by implication, against France. By 1873 he had formed them into an élite club: the League of Three Emperors. Out of the agony of France he conjured not only a united Germany, but a Germany guaranteed by the most powerful alliance in Europe.

He wanted neither war nor democracy, but that things should stay as they were – which they did for the next twenty years. During these years he bound the imperial partners closer together by a web of treaties: an Insurance Treaty with Austria in case of aggression by Russia; a Reinsurance Treaty with Russia as a protection against any rash step by Austria, particularly in the Balkans. 'One day the great European war will come out of some damn foolish thing in the Balkans,' he prophesied. 'Then all Europe will be engulfed, and the Socialists will take over and destroy what the armies have not.' It was a prediction of frightening accuracy, and he made sure that it would not be fulfilled in his lifetime.

These were years of headlong growth of both population and industry in Europe, which the old systems of government were poorly designed to handle; but the Germans prospered under their Iron Chancellor, who gave them the advanced social legislation of a welfare state, not so much out of regard for the masses as in order to keep the political initiative in his own hands. 'A man who can look forward to a pension is far more contented and easier to manage than one who can't,' he said. 'Men are like animals – they're contented so long as they're secure and well-fed.'

Although the German Social Democrats were the foremost socialist group in Europe, they were not yet a challenging political force. Even moderate liberals were condemned to permanent opposition. They had only one champion of real standing – the Crown Prince – and he was as firmly excluded from government in the new régime as he had been in the old. He could only wait for his father to die.

'Poor Fritz is inclined to despond,' Vicky wrote, and he had cause; Wilhelm lived on to be eighty and then ninety, apparently indestructible. 'Sometimes I think our chance will never come,' Fritz confessed to her. 'When we married I imagined that we would lead the country in peace and enlightenment. I little thought, when I brought you here, that it would be for these twenty-five miserable and useless years.' His own constitution was not strong; he suffered from colds and lack of energy; he still looked magnificent, but as a figurehead he was beginning to fade.

Nor was he pleased with his heir. Willy had grown from a wilful boy into an insufferable young man, with few signs of the qualities of statesmanship. 'I think there's a great deal in him,' his mother wrote to hers. 'If one can root out pride, conceitedness, selfishness and laziness he may be a fine character some day.' But as he grew so did the gulf between Willy and his parents. He left home, first as a student, then as a cadet in the army, then to set up his own household after an early marriage to Princess Augusta Victoria of Schleswig-Holstein-Sonderburg–

Willy as a student in Bonn

Willy with his wife, Augusta Victoria

Augustenburg, a large, placid, fertile girl, known in the family as Dona – 'the cow from Holstein', Bismarck called her.

One feels that, like many unsatisfactory children, Willy was anxious to do right; he was certainly determined to do well, and looked forward to being a worthy successor to Frederick the Great. Devotion to his grandfather – Wilhelm, not Albert – pride in the army, and the influence of Bismarck identified him with the forces opposing his father – of whose ineffectiveness he was contemptuous – and turned him violently against his mother, whose strong will and dogmatic manner infuriated him.

Bismarck was partially responsible for their estrangement. The old Kaiser could not last much longer, and when Fritz succeeded to the throne the Chancellor would be faced with an Emperor whose policies were anathema to him and who might even dispense with his services. His best defence against that was clearly the creation of a strong opposing faction led by the next Crown Prince. He therefore cultivated and flattered the young Wilhelm and encouraged the aged one to do the same. He was also determined that Vicky should have no influence over her son.

When Bismarck arranged for the young man to have access to the Foreign Office – a privilege which the Crown Prince had never been accorded – both Fritz and Vicky protested; but as usual, in vain. In 1885 Willy was sent on a ceremonial visit to St Petersburg, in preference to his father. The Tsar found him 'an arrogant young man'; but Willy returned with the impression that he had won the Tsar's heart: 'He looks upon me as a son'.

Kaiser Wilhelm was ninety in March 1887 and Fritz made a speech at his birthday dinner in a voice which was noticeably hoarse. Fritz then took to his bed for a couple of weeks, but at the end of that time his throat was still inflamed and he could hardly speak. The Professor of Medicine from Berlin University found a small growth on the vocal chords, which grew steadily. Other doctors arrived, diagnosed cancer and proposed to operate without consulting either the patient or the Emperor. In the meantime they tried cauterising the tumour daily with red-hot wires, an ordeal which Fritz bore with great bravery. It seems likely that he suspected from then on that his case was mortal and for the next year faced in silence and with impressive fortitude the double tragedy of a painful and early death and the collapse of all his long-frustrated political hopes. It was possible that he might not outlive his father, and as the news got around a macabre *opéra bouffe* was performed about the speechless and tragic figure of the Crown Prince.

Bismarck was perturbed: the old Emperor was failing at last, and Willy had recently alarmed the Chancellor by talking wildly of colonies and navies; the prospect of having a rash young man as his new master, rather than as a pawn in the continuing political game, inclined him to hope that Fritz might, after all, be the next Kaiser. 'I found royalty in a bad way,' he wrote to his wife. 'Now and then I fancy I have been the means of making it a little too powerful.' He made plans to control Fritz, forbade the operation and insisted on an outside opinion.

Vicky was relieved and surprised by Bismarck's concern, and found him suddenly, and briefly, 'very nice'. Her youthful, spontaneous cheerfulness had long since gone; she remained bright and energetic, but she had already been through a good deal and her trials had left her brittle and irritable. The bitterness of dead hopes ate deeply into her; nevertheless in the last year of Fritz's life she devoted herself more completely than ever to him, and tried to appear hopeful.

In May, Victoria sent an English throat specialist, Dr Morell Mackenzie, off to Berlin, where he immediately pronounced the growth benign and curable without operation. The Crown Prince and Princess were understandably delighted, but their German doctors, while relieved to have so much responsibility removed from their shoulders, remained sceptical and said so. Rumours began to circulate and became grotesque: that Britain was plotting the death of the Crown Prince; that the Princess was concealing his true state in order that she might act as Regent; that she and Mackenzie were lovers, united in a bid for power. Bismarck did nothing to refute them and Willy – from confused motives of his own – subscribed to the general calumny of his mother. Fritz, who though dumb was not deaf, was extremely distressed, and both he and Vicky longed to leave Germany.

Their wish coincided with Queen Victoria's Golden Jubilee, and on 12 June 1887 they left for London, to take part in the celebrations and attend Dr Mackenzie's clinic. Fritz's health was now generally undermined and he had to rest a great deal; but he enjoyed the Jubilee and rode in the procession, a commanding figure in white uniform that put his English relatives in mind of Lohengrin. 'At half-past eleven we left the Palace, I driving in a handsomely gilt landau drawn by six of the Creams, with dear Vicky and Alix,' Victoria recorded in her diary. 'Dear Fritz looked so handsome.'

From London, Fritz went with Vicky to Osborne, where he felt better and regained some vestige of his voice. From Osborne they moved to Scotland, which was too damp, and then to Toblach in the Tyrol, which was too cold, and to Bavero in Italy, which was too humid. In November they settled into a villa at San Remo. There Crown Prince Rudolf – the Heir to Austria-Hungary – came to see them. He was a contemporary of Willy, whom he did not like, and full of charm and liberal sentiments: 'so filial, so kind and such a contrast to Willy,' Vicky wrote.

Their absence from Berlin was not appreciated in Germany, for the old Kaiser was obviously dying. He lay on his camp bed in his almost unfurnished room, too weak to move without help, and wandered in his mind: sometimes he thought Willy was his son. Bismarck continued to govern, with the young Wilhelm

Queen Victoria's Golden Jubilee celebrations in 1887

deputed to sign for his grandfather – a practical enough arrangement which infuriated Vicky and hurt Fritz. When he visited his
parents at San Remo, in the belief that his father was in bad
hands and that he himself should take control, Willy instantly
quarrelled with his mother. 'He was as rude, as disagreeable and
as impertinent to me as possible when he arrived, but I pitched
into him with, I am afraid, considerable violence,' Vicky wrote to
Victoria. 'He spoke before others and half turning his back to
me, so I said I would go and tell his father how he behaved and
ask that he should be forbidden the house.' Willy returned to
Berlin, and the breach between them never healed; from then on
he was his mother's enemy.

By then Fritz was very ill. His voice had gone again for good,
he had grown thinner and weaker, and his throat was so painful
that ice-bags had to be applied constantly to it. In November the
doctors converged on him again, and Mackenzie admitted that
the disease was a cancer and far advanced: he was not expected
to live through the following year. Rather than risk the cold of a
Berlin winter, he and Vicky remained in San Remo, in isolation
and distress.

Kaiser Wilhelm I died in March 1888, at the age of ninety-one,
holding the portrait of his youthful and long dead love, Elisa
Radziwill, with whom he presumably hoped to be reunited.
While still coherent, he had reached up to touch Bismarck's
hand, saying, 'You have done well, Bismarck. I've always been
pleased with you. You've always done the right thing.' Bismarck
wept.

When the news reached San Remo, Fritz put on his uniform,
removed the insignia of the Black Eagle from his chest and laid it
on Vicky's, wrote on the pad which was now his only means of
communication a note of thanks to Mackenzie for keeping him
alive long enough to be Emperor, and set out for Berlin. He
styled himself Kaiser Frederick III and tried to rule, retaining
Bismarck as Chancellor and reading and writing state papers in
his apartments; but he was a spent force. The country was
waiting for Willy, who did not conceal his impatience to inherit
the throne. Bismarck, adjusting his defences to the new situation,
behaved as the true head of government, treating the new
Emperor with formal correctness, Crown Prince Wilhelm with a
brusqueness calculated to keep him in his place, and Vicky –
whose influence he still feared – with open hostility. Vicky

Wilhelm I lying in state in the Cathedral at Berlin

Mourning parade for Wilhelm I in Berlin

Fritz as Emperor Frederick III

The funeral of Frederick III in Potsdam

nursed and protected Fritz under increasing strain and he survived for another ninety anguished days: after a lifetime of waiting, he reigned for just three months, and died on 15 June 1888.

Wilhelm's first act as Kaiser was to seal off his parents' palace with troops and ransack it for his father's papers, which he suspected Vicky of hiding. In fact, she had already sent them to England, so the search was fruitless, and Vicky was left with nothing but grief. 'It seems as if I had seen a fine, noble ship sink at sea, with all the nation's hopes, its freedom, its progress,' she wrote, and retired into widowhood, reluctantly abandoning the task given her by her father thirty years before. It may be doubted whether Fritz would in any circumstances have been a great Emperor, for he was not a strong personality or a man of outstanding talent; but at least he was committed to a style of government very different from that which followed.

Bismarck went back to his estate without waiting for the funeral. Whether he underestimated Kaiser Wilhelm II or whether his own powers were failing (one of his sons made the Wagnerian comment: 'My father can no longer wield the hammer'), Bismarck chose to maintain the maximum distance, and therefore the minimum friction, between himself and his new sovereign. Wilhelm, at twenty-nine, was as determined to master his empire as his mother had been for him to overcome the disability of his withered arm when he was a boy; the two circumstances were connected, and from this connection Wilhelm had developed a sense of inferiority which impelled him towards intemperate words and policies.

Although foolish, he was not stupid; he had a quick and restless mind and was superficially interested in everything. His future Chancellor, Caprivi – who was to follow Bismarck – had already asked, 'Whatever will happen if Prince Wilhelm becomes Kaiser now? He thinks he understands *everything,* even ship-building.' It was as though his maternal grandfather's sober breadth of interests had run wild. 'His Majesty has dramatic rather than political instincts,' Baron von Holstein – the *eminence grise* of the German Foreign Office – observed; and Bismarck complained, 'This new Emperor is like a balloon. If you don't keep fast hold of the string you never know where he'll be off to.'

Within weeks of his accession he was off to St Petersburg and returned convinced that Russian strength was aimed against him, and that new alliances should be made against her and German power increased. The delicate weighting by which Bismarck had kept Europe in balance was ignored. Crown Prince Rudolf of Austria wrote to the Prince of Wales, 'The Kaiser is likely to cause great confusion in Europe before long. He is just the man for it.' The British agreed; Lord Salisbury added his own to the many epigrams Wilhelm was to attract: '*There* is the dark cloud.'

Wilhelm's adulation of the German army was absolute, and his first official statement as Emperor – on receiving its oath of allegiance – anticipated the entire course of his reign: 'We belong to each other – I and the army – we were born for each other and will cleave indissolubly to each other, whether it be the will of God to send us calm or storm.' He could equally well have said that he and Germany were born for each other. Berlin was waiting for such a Kaiser: 'Almost every Platz sported a colossal

Bismarck with Wilhelm II, 30 October 1888

group of statuary honouring military achievements. . . . If imperial Paris had been a monument to French civilisation, imperial Berlin was to be a monument to Prussian militarism.'[1] He added to its splendour a grandiosely refurbished court with flunkeys dressed in the court uniform of Frederick the Great, a gold-and-white royal train, a royal yacht, and whatever appurtenances of majesty came to his quick and shifting brain.

All the same, he was an intensely moral man, dominating his family with Lutheran severity, and he strongly disapproved of the loose ways of his Uncle Bertie, the English Prince of Wales. The antipathy was mutual and was to have unhappy consequences.

At the beginning of his reign he received some credit for championing the workers – 'I want to be king of the poor as well as the rich,' he said; but his attitude was entirely paternalistic and his horror of socialism as great as Bismarck's. The prefix he chose for himself was The All-Highest: he was as certain as any other autocrat that the crown came to him from God, and a perspicacious god at that; moreover, to him a nation was an army, 'the people are the troops and I am their commander-in-chief'. Kingship was a duty which he accepted briskly: 'The man who finds himself at the helm must act.'

Wilhelm possessed one other dominating and fatal characteristic – his 'fluency in speaking meant that he approached all questions with an open mouth'.[2] Holstein soon noticed that 'the more important a matter is the more it interests him, and he talks more rapidly and incautiously'; and when he took to talking at length to the subordinate members of his Council of Ministers, Bismarck was moved to invoke a decree of 1852 which forbade any discussion between the monarch and members of his Council without the knowledge of the Chief Minister.

The issue itself was trivial, but Bismarck went to Berlin to fight for his position. Wilhelm objected, quite reasonably, that he could not always consult a Chancellor who hid in the country; but Bismarck insisted and insulted the Kaiser in front of the Council, a sin which was not forgiven. Wilhelm, an earlier bird than Bismarck, visited the Chancellory at the beginning of one morning and caught Bismarck off-balance, unshaved and plagued with neuralgia. At the climax of their altercation, Bis-

Wilhelm II

marck threw his papers on to the floor and told Wilhelm to govern without him; but he had chosen the wrong Wilhelm. Realising his mistake, the old Chancellor went down on his knees and picked up the papers, leaving only one – a personal letter from the Tsar, which Wilhelm demanded to see. It described himself: 'a badly brought-up boy of ill will'. He demanded Bismarck's resignation and left.

Bismarck, looking around for help, found that everyone – parliament, colleagues, court – had had enough of him. He even made a despairing appeal to Vicky, who told him, 'You yourself have destroyed my influence with my son. I can do nothing.' He caught the train from Berlin into oblivion: the Bismarckian age ended as abruptly as it had begun.

Chapter six

Revolutionaries and Rudolf

Although liberalism and even prudence had gone under in Germany, German revolutionary philosophy was alive and well and had until recently been living in London in the person of Karl Marx. Marx had been forced out of Germany after the 1848 rebellions, in which he had played a part, along with Engels, who became his lifelong collaborator in formulating the great nineteenth-century basis of communist doctrine, which they misleadingly called dialectical materialism.

Their philosophical starting-point had been the work of Hegel, the pre-eminent German thinker whose vision of a human social Ideal had somehow turned into the formidable concept of the Prussian State. Marx moved on from this static Ideal to the notion that human society evolved continuously out of practical necessity (he was a contemporary of Darwin), and that the strongest pressures in this process were economic. As the Industrial Revolution spread across Europe, creating a new relationship of classes, Marx opposed to the *thesis* of Hegelian authority the *antithesis* of the workers' revolution and proposed, as the outcome of their struggle, the *synthesis* of a communist world society.

In 1847 he wrote, with Engels, *The Communist Manifesto,* which ended with the famous exhortation: 'Let the ruling classes tremble at the prospect of a communist revolution. Proletarians have nothing to lose but their chains. They have a world to win. Proletarians of all lands, unite!' Like Lenin after him, he was a

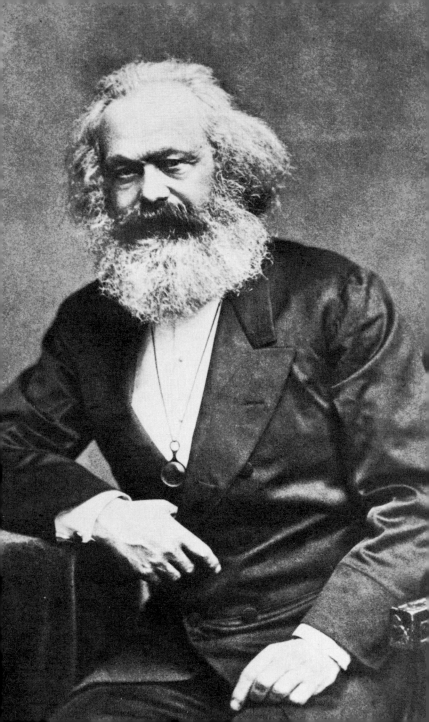

Friedrich Engels

firm believer in centrally organised action, and in 1864 helped to found the International Working Men's Association, known subsequently as the First International. In 1867 he published the first volume of *Das Kapital*.

Communism was by no means a new goal, but the old roads to it were less clearly mapped. The French Revolution was inspired by the vaguer ideals of liberty, equality and fraternity, and the methods of the earlier revolutionists tended to be based on the spontaneous anarchy of brotherhood. That tradition, continued in the writing of Proudhon, inspired Lasalle, the first notable demagogue of German socialism, and also Bakunin and the

Karl Marx

Russian Narodniks, who assassinated Tsar Alexander II in 1881, and – above all – the Paris Commune of 1871; but when old Delescluze mounted his last barricade in his Communard uniform, and was shot down, the main revolutionary initiative passed into Marxist hands. 'Working-man's Paris, with its Commune, will be celebrated for ever as the glorious harbinger of a new society,' Marx wrote, and it certainly was.

Vicky read Marx with interest and sent her secretary, the younger Stockmar, to check up on him. Stockmar reported that Marx spoke of her with 'due respect and propriety' and did not appear to be a trouble-maker; yet communism was the liberals' enemy, not their ally. From then on there were always three main bodies of opinion in European political thought: the reactionaries, who stood for dynastic institutions and their privileges; the constitutional liberals, who represented the advancing bourgeoisie and wanted a freer hand within a moderately reformed society; and the socialists, who demanded that society be completely redrawn. The divisions blurred from time to time, and the factions fared variously in different countries, but a triangular fight was joined that would not be over until the last emperor fell.

In 1888 the forces of reaction were firmly in control in Russia, where there was no thought of a parliament, and in Germany and Austria-Hungary, which possessed nominal parliaments without power. The fate of liberalism, sealed in Germany by the death of Frederick III, was not yet decided, however, in Austria. Although Franz Josef's experiment in 'a little parliamentarianism' ended at Sadowa in 1866, liberal groups within the Austrian Empire were still strong and looked hopefully towards their own Crown Prince.

When he was only fifteen, Rudolf had written, 'Monarchy is now a mighty ruin which may remain from today till tomorrow, but which will ultimately tumble. It has stood for centuries and as long as the people could be led blindly it was good, but now its task is over, all people are free and the next storm will bring the ruin tumbling down.' By the time he was twenty he was known as a free-thinker who despised the aristocracy, and the one man who might lead the Hapsburg Empire out of its otherwise hopeless *impasse;* but now, at thirty-five, he was an enigmatic and uncertain character.

As a small boy he had been beset by alarming tutors chosen by

Crown Prince Rudolf

the Archduchess Sophie to instil him with courage. He had had revolvers fired close to his head, had been locked in a maze with an imagined wild boar, and was encouraged to shoot at anything that moved, including the finches outside his nursery window. Elizabeth had rescued him, only to turn him over to her pet pedants who tried to fill his young mind with encyclopaedic knowledge. He was a bright boy and in appearance like his mother – charming, graceful and handsome – but mentally and physically fragile. He grew up to have little in common with his father except an equal love of hunting and women; for his temperament he was more indebted to Elizabeth and the fact that his parents' marriage was the twenty-second alliance between the houses of Hapsburg and Wittelsbach. Inbreeding gave him, among other things, a gothic sense of morbidity. 'My brain seethes and works away all day; no sooner has one thought gone than another takes its place. Each one compels me, each one says something different, now gay and cheerful, now raven black with rage,' he wrote, and he confided to his publisher friend, Szeps: 'From time to time I try to find an opportunity of seeing a dying man and eavesdropping on his last breath.'

Behind his enviable public image there lay a private life of agonising instability: he drank a lot, took drugs, and was so desperately active and indiscriminating a lover that by his mid-thirties he was faced with impotence and syphilis. 'Female hearts positively dropped into the lap of the Crown Prince,' a member of the German embassy noticed, 'but his body was not up to the demands he made on it'. The same was true of his mind: 'Rudolf was not a genius; he was a dynast who saw too much, who asked too much of himself.'[1]

He was devoted to his mother, and she to him, and Franz Josef was fond and proud of him in an uncomprehending, undemonstrative way; but they were a divided family. The Emperor and Empress were now known to be sexually estranged, Elizabeth spending long periods away from Vienna and Franz Josef now permanently consoled by a plump and intelligent actress, Katherina Schratt, whom he installed in a villa near the palace. Early in the morning he would walk across the park to take breakfast with her, before settling to another long day at his desk. In 1881 he forced Rudolf into a dynastic marriage to the plain, dull but conveniently Catholic daughter of the King of the Belgians. Rudolf was unfaithful to her and gave her syphilis, with the result that she was never able to produce an heir. By 1888 Rudolf was trying to divorce her.

He was given no share in government, and remained 'a quiet observer, close to the hubbub of political life without intervening in it';[2] yet politically he was not unimportant. He believed that the future of Austria lay in the Danube Basin and in the Balkans, where the collapse of the Turkish empire was leaving a danger-ous vacuum, and, like Bismarck, he guessed correctly that the next crucial struggle for power would be over the Balkans and their Slavic peoples. 'The Slavs, to whatever nation they belong, have a mighty future,' he wrote. 'Only by cultivating the Slavs can Russian influence be paralysed.'

He soon became a centre of hope not only for the liberals but also for the national minorities of his father's empire. He visited Prague and spoke in their own language to the Czechs; above all, however, he inherited his mother's love of Hungary and became the figurehead of the Magyar separatists, who longed to depose Franz Josef from the Hungarian throne and make Rudolf their king. A plan for a *coup d'état* was drawn around him and, although he rejected it, intolerable pressure was put on him. 'God knows, I am not ambitious,' he wrote to his old tutor. 'My views, allegiance, obedience and wisdom are greater than my vanity. If I wanted to play a bad, an evil part, to become a rebel, I could do so on the greatest and most far-reaching scale – indeed, I am being offered the part from all sides.'

Vienna itself, under its crust of imperial formality, was a ferment of new ideas. It was the time of Freud and Adler, of Bruckner and Hugo Wolf, of a vivid, multi-racial *fin-du-siècle* society in which prostitution and perversion, corruption and brilliance, commerce and finance, poetry and death were fascinatingly mixed: a toxic emulsion in which Rudolf swam and then drowned.

Among the suspect *élite* of cosmopolitan intellectuals was a family of international financiers, the Baltazzis, who came from Constantinople. One particularly luscious Baltazzi married an Austrian diplomat and became Baroness Helene Vetsera, and by 1888 their daughter Marie was Rudolf's mistress. Marie was eighteen, plump and attractive, 'with a seductive and irresistible grace'. Since leaving convent she had already had one wild *affaire* in Egypt and was obviously made for loving. 'Both of us lost our heads, now we belong to each other body and soul,' she wrote soon after she met Rudolf.

To what extent what happened to them both was premeditated will presumably never be known. It seems most likely that the strong currents surging through Rudolf – his intense morbidity, his fear of the future, the overwhelming claims of dynasty and the effects of disease – were suddenly too much for him. On 30 January 1889 he left the bed of the *grande cocotte* of Vienna, Mitzi Hauser, and was driven by his cabbie Bratfisch across the ice and snow to the Imperial hunting-lodge at Mayerling, where Marie was waiting for him. The next morning he and Marie were found in his bedroom, both naked and both dead. Marie lay on the bed with a red rose in her pubic hair and a bullet-hole in her forehead. What was left of Rudolf was propped beside her: the top of his head was blown off. There was a little champagne left, and a lot of blood and a suicide note.

Marie Vetsera

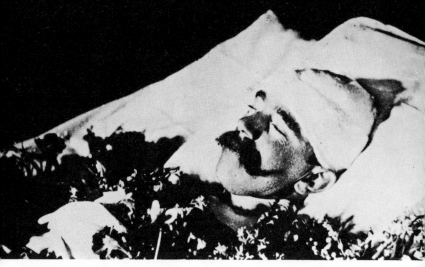

Rudolf after death

Extraordinary measures were taken to conceal the event. The guest who had found them, together with a servant, cleared up the mess and hid Marie's body in an attic. Rudolf's corpse, its topless head heavily bandaged, was returned to Vienna, where it was announced that he had taken his life while alone and of unsound mind. The following night, Marie's two Baltazzi uncles were sent to Mayerling to take her away. They dressed her stiff body, frog-marched it to their carriage and drove away with it seated between them as though alive. It was buried secretly at the Cistercian abbey at Heiligenkreuz.

In spite of these ghoulish precautions, the truth was soon widely known; yet not only the Emperor and Empress but most of Austria-Hungary grieved for their Crown Prince. Whatever Rudolf's real nature and potential, a light had indeed failed. The new Heir Apparent was an unlikeable autocrat, Franz Josef's nephew, the Archduke Franz Ferdinand. Neither Slavs nor Magyars, liberals nor minorities anywhere in Central Europe could see any hope of a voluntary breaking of imperial reaction, and organised socialism was by no means ready to challenge it. The order for the future was clearly to be of autocracy tempered by assassination, in the Russian pattern.

Alexander III

Chapter seven

Nicky and Alix

All this time Russia hung behind the European stage like a dark but jewelled backcloth. The Great Russian state, centred on Moscow, had arisen out of the Tatar wars, and the Romanovs had ruled it for nearly three hundred years. It had grown steadily until it stretched from eastern Europe to the Pacific. At the beginning of the eighteenth century Peter the Great moved the capital from Moscow to St Petersburg, which he built in a style of grey classicism on the marshes at the mouth of the Neva river, in the far north-west, as 'a window on Europe'; but the Tsars of all the Russias remained the supreme autocrats of an undeveloped and sparsely inhabited sub-continent. For all that, the Romanovs ruled some hundred and thirty million people – Russians, Ukrainians, Poles, Tatars, Mongols and others – by the end of the nineteenth century, and the Tsar was still as remote as, and closely identified with, God.

For the Orthodox Church was descended from Byzantium: when Constantinople fell to the infidels at the end of the middle ages, the Tsars became its champions and were themselves endowed with the messianic glory and mystery of the true faith. Little Father Tsar was the head of the church as well as of the state, and stood, supreme and alone, between his people and their maker. All power of government was vested in him, and so was all wealth: the golden splendours of his capital, profane and sacred, were the heaven-on-earth of a dark land where multitudes lived nearly as close to nature as animals. His will was

Alexander II

imposed across thousands of almost trackless miles by a corrupt and inefficient bureaucracy and a corrupt and powerful police force.

The vast cruelties of Ivan the Terrible and Catherine the Great were horrors of the past, but Russia was still a barbarous despotism, almost untouched by European thought. Throughout the whole of the nineteenth century there was no major social advance within the Empire, except the emancipation of the serfs by Alexander II in 1861. Twenty years later, on 13 March 1881, the same Tsar drafted a Ukase* giving effect to very tentative reforms, and was assassinated on his way to sign it. His son and successor, Alexander III, cancelled the Ukase.

Alexander III was a huge and strong man, slow of thought, ponderously authoritarian, and as obstinately and traditionally Russian as a bear. The only reformist groups which faced him were the scattered terrorists of the Narodnaya Volya – 'The

* An imperial decree.

The assassination of Alexander II

People's Will' – who were drawn from the tiny intelligentsia of the cities but based their revolutionary idealism on their belief in the 'instinctive socialism' of the peasants. They had no organisation and made themselves felt only by isolated acts of political murder. In 1887 an attempt on the life of the Tsar was made by a group of Narodniks which included a student named Alexander Ulyanov, who was hanged. From then on, repression was even more severe and Alexander III lived under heavy guard.

Alexander distrusted not only Kaiser Wilhelm II, but Germany, and Europe, and most European ideas except the concepts of industrialism, into which he was persuaded by his only progressive minister, Sergius Witte. Whole factory areas were added to the cities, linked by railroads, funded by foreign capital (some British and German, but mainly French), and attracted a labour force of some sixteen millions from the villages. The small nuclei of a liberal middle class and an urban proletariat were born, though as yet without self-awareness or self-expression. None of it altered the lives of the rural masses, which were in fact made harder by successive bad harvests.

All new wealth, like all the old, belonged ultimately to the Tsar, and immediately to the aristocrats and industrialists and financiers who surrounded the court. In the 1890s Moscow and St Petersburg were boom towns, where the *beau monde* spoke French. The Tsarina – the Empress Marie, a Danish princess and sister of Alexandra, the wife of the Prince of Wales – shone and glittered at the centre of society, and lesser royalty rotated around her; but the Tsar kept aloof and continued to govern as though nothing were changing.

Alexander III as Tsarevich, with his wife Marie and their son Nicholas

Alexander's only recorded gesture to the west is an extraordinary one. France had obstinately refused to lie down after the trials of 1871, and under its mediocre and bourgeois Third Republic had become again a powerful, rich and civilised state, heavily subsidising – among other things – Russia's belated industrial revolution. Closer ties were clearly desirable, and in 1891 French warships visited Kronstadt, the naval base near St Petersburg, and there his Imperial Majesty Tsar Alexander III actually stood to attention for the playing of the *Marseillaise*. The following year, a military pact was signed between the two countries: in Paris and St Petersburg almost any alliance was palatable in the face of the new Germany.

At about this time, Alexander began to look to the future in another context: his eldest son, the heir to the Tsardom, was twenty-four and it seemed time to think of his marriage. The Tsarevich Nicholas was in almost every way a contrast to his father: he was a rather short young man, slight and blue-eyed, with a certain diffident charm. Since finishing his education he had been enjoying the life – described by Tolstoy as 'of obligatory and unimpeachable idleness' – of an army officer. Stationed near St Petersburg, he took part in parades, got drunk at 'merry' dinners with his fellow officers, and was a frequent visitor to the ballet and the opera, and a guest at parties which went on afterwards until dawn. He was an agreeable companion within the circle of his acquaintance – and it would never have occurred to him to step outside it. He liked to be liked, and to this end usually agreed with people – though he had a disconcerting habit of changing his mind with his company.

For a year or two he had had a flirtation with a young star of the ballet, Mathilde Kschessinska, and would sit in her dressing-room before the theatre and take her for starlit rides in his troika afterwards. In the summer of 1892 he set her up in a small house in St Petersburg, riding there every evening in time for supper. It was a pleasant existence. The routine and lack of responsibility of the military life were just what appealed to his weak-willed nature; within it, he did not feel inadequate.

Nicholas took little interest in the affairs of state. The few minor duties he was given bored him; ministers met a frightening coldness beneath the charm. Alexander's attitude to his son was one of mild contempt. 'Have you ever had a serious conversation with the Heir about anything?' he asked Witte in exasperation.

Alexander III with his wife, the Empress Marie, and their children (from left) Michael, Nicholas, Olga, Xenia and George

'He is still absolutely a child, he has infantile judgments.' He himself made no attempt to bridge the gap between Nicholas and his delayed maturity. He was in his forties, in the prime of health and vigour. Neither he nor Nicky (as he was known in the family) could conceive of a time when he would not be ruling Russia. To Nicky, the idea of ever having to assume this stupendous responsibility himself was a distant nightmare outside the scope of his imagination.

Nicky and Alix

Mathilde Kschessinska   *Grand Duke Serge*

He was also little interested in the idea of marriage, and was much relieved when his father's tentative overtures in the directions of European princesses were refused, on religious grounds. Nicholas maintained with the steady obstinacy of a mild temperament that, if and when he was married, it could only be to Princess Alix of Hesse-Darmstadt. This choice his parents opposed. They did not want a German match; moreover, the young princess had personally made a poor impression when she came to St Petersburg in 1889 to visit her sister, who was married to Nicholas's uncle Serge. Shy and gauche, speaking French with a strong German accent, she was not, they thought, of the stuff of which future Empresses are made.

With the question of his marriage at a standstill, Nicky went to London in the summer of 1893 to represent his parents at the marriage of his cousin George (later George V) to Princess Mary of Teck. His English relations were pleased to find that the heir to the mysterious Romanovs looked 'very like Georgie'. In fact, his likeness to his cousin was the cause of several farcical mistakes in identity. Queen Victoria – who more than half a century before had danced with his grandfather and fallen a little in love with him – gave him lunch and the Order of the Garter, and the Prince of Wales, after one look at Nicholas's clothes, recommended a tailor, a hatter and a bootmaker.

Nicholas II as Tsarevich   *Empress Alexandra in about 1895*

That winter, Alexander III fell ill; an attack of influenza led to serious kidney trouble. Illness was a new experience to this formidably strong man, and brought a frightening reminder that he was mortal. Suddenly, the securing of the succession became of urgent importance, and the question of Nicholas's betrothal was raised again. In the spring, he was to visit Hesse-Darmstadt. The occasion was the marriage of the young Grand Duke of Hesse-Darmstadt to his cousin 'Ducky', one of Victoria's many granddaughters. Nicholas was to represent his parents at the wedding. Before he went, he obtained their consent to his proposal to the Grand Duke's sister, Alix.

A generation earlier, the heir to the Grand Duchy of Hesse-Darmstadt had been considered by some a poor match for Queen Victoria's second daughter, Alice. But the Prince Consort – himself a native of Coburg – naturally looked to the small German states to provide good husbands for his daughters. That carefully prearranged 'love match' had been one of his last achievements. In Darmstadt Alice was within the same country

Nicholas and Alix before their marriage

as her sister Vicky; but family relations were badly strained by the Austro–Prussian war of 1866. Hesse-Darmstadt, fighting on the side of Austria, was defeated and made to pay a large indemnity, which impoverished both the country and the Royal family personally. Alice's health suffered, and when diphtheria swept through the family a few years later, she quickly succumbed and died, leaving a young family of seven children.

Alix was one of the youngest. She was only six when the sudden deaths of her mother and younger sister cast the first, perhaps long-lasting shadows on an emotional temperament. She grew up to be a quiet, shy girl; the smile which had earned her the nickname 'Sunny' was rarely seen outside the family circle. Queen Victoria took a special interest in this motherless family, and as far as possible directed its upbringing by remote control from England. Their English governess sent regular reports to Windsor: Mrs Orchard, in charge of the nursery, was as solid and English as her name. The Grand Duke's children ate their rice pudding and baked apples with the same regularity as their English cousins, in rooms filled with portraits of English relations and watercolours of English scenes.

Alix had twice travelled from her tiny enclosed country to Russia: at the age of twelve she had attended her older sister Ella's wedding to the Grand Duke Serge, where the sixteen-year-old Nicholas was also a guest. Five years later she visited her married sister in St Petersburg, skated and danced with the Tsarevich, and fell in love with him. But she felt it was a hopeless love: at sixteen she had been confirmed into the Lutheran church, and religion was at the solemn core of her life.

Alix was now twenty-two, tall and beautiful in an angular, Grecian style. With her elder sisters married, she had been hostess for her brother for the past two years. Now that he was to be married, the cobbled streets of the medieval town of Darmstadt rang with the carriage wheels of royalty arriving from all over Europe. Queen Victoria was making the journey from England to see her grandchildren married. So was the Prince of Wales, 'Uncle Bertie' – always a genial, tactful guest at family weddings. From Prussia Kaiser Wilhelm, with a dazzling variety of uniforms, and his mother Vicky, the widowed Empress Frederick, who now devoted her unquenchable energy to gardening and collecting objets d'art. There was a posse of girl cousins with practically indistinguishable pet names – Missy, Mossy, Louie,

Sossy – all prepared to discuss endlessly the romance which hung in the air, almost eclipsing the wedding.

The day after his arrival, Nicholas proposed, and was steadfastly refused by a weeping Alix. Then the family went into action: Alix had already refused an English prince and must not be allowed to waste another opportunity. Queen Victoria had a talk to her, and so did her sister Ella. The Kaiser, who thought German influence might be reinforced at the Russian court, also gave his advice to both Alix and Nicky. It was he who – immediately the wedding celebrations were over – led Nicholas to the door of Alix's sitting-room, put a bouquet of flowers into his hands, and waited with other relations in the next room, while Nicky plied his suit once more.

This time Nicholas was successful. 'With her first words she consented,' he wrote to his mother. She was his 'darling, adorable Alix'. He was 'in Paradise' and surrounded by approving congratulations. Telegrams poured in, and from Russia the Empress sent her future daughter-in-law a jewelled bracelet and the invitation to call her 'Mother Dear'.

After ten delightful days they parted – to meet a month later in England. They first stayed with Alix's eldest sister, Princess Victoria of Battenberg, at Walton-on-Thames – a June idyll of boating, picnicking and exchanging confidences under the bells of the summer trees. Nicky confessed to his liaison with Kschessinska – now at an end – and Alix had the pleasure of forgiving him. The Love of a Good Woman was rated high in that era. She appointed herself his Guardian Angel. Nicholas found himself enfolded in a love so intense and possessive that he was sometimes to feel his response was inadequate.

At the end of July, after some weeks at Windsor and Osborne with 'Granny', Nicholas had to return to Russia. He found his family anxious again over the Tsar's health. Soon Alexander took to his bed in his summer palace of Livadia in the Crimea, and despite the doctors' ministrations and the priests' prayers, he grew worse. Nicholas, with a terrible sense of his approaching fate, sent for his fiancée.

Alix set out at once, travelling by train through the huge, alien country as an ordinary passenger; there had been no time to make any special arrangements. The Tsar received her as he felt a Tsar should – in full dress uniform. But, having given his official blessing on the betrothal, he returned to bed, a dying man. The

Empress Marie took charge, and the future Tsar hung around in the background, waiting for news. Alix was quickly alert to the situation. She urged Nicholas to assert himself, and 'make the doctors come first to you'. A new influence had arrived at the palace.

On 1 November 1894 Alexander died, and his appalled son found himself Tsar and Emperor of All the Russias – a fate for which he knew himself to be hopelessly inadequate. He was twenty-six, but sounded more like a schoolboy in his anguished appeal to his brother-in-law: 'What am I going to do? . . . I am not prepared to be a Tsar. I know nothing of the business of ruling.'

The next morning, Alix was received into the Orthodox faith, an ardent convert. She had now become 'the truly believing Alexandra Fedorovna'. Nicky felt he could not face the future without his 'Sunny' at his side. A week after the funeral they were married in St Petersburg. That night Alix wrote in her husband's diary, 'At last united, bound for life. . . . Yours, yours.'

A few weeks later, Nicky received a delegation from the *zemstva* – local councils, almost the only elected bodies in Russia – to offer their formal congratulations on his accession. His speech in reply was to be the first official pronouncement of his reign, and was awaited with interest and some hope by the liberal elements in the country. Little was known of the new Tsar's personality, but his youth and gentle manner suggested that the new reign might not be so rigidly autocratic as his father's. His speech must have sent a chill into their hearts. The delegates heard the slight young man read, in his pleasant voice, 'It is known to me that voices have been heard in some *zemstvo* assemblies of persons carried away by senseless dreams of the participation of *zemstvo* representatives in the affairs of internal government. Let all know that . . . I shall preserve the principle of autocracy as firmly and undeviatingly as did my father.'

The speech had probably been written for him, but the sentiments were his. At the heart of his timid, vacillating personality was an inflexible belief in his divine rights as a ruler. As a boy of thirteen he had watched his grandfather, 'the Tsar-liberator', die, mutilated by a revolutionary's bomb. This horrifying memory served to underline the importance of not giving away an inch to the dark and terrifying forces of change at work beneath the surface of Russian life.

Nicholas II and Alexandra in their coronation robes

The first year of Nicholas's reign and of his marriage passed quietly – it was a time of official mourning. Towards the end of it Alix gave birth to their first child, a daughter, Olga. Domestic life suited the new Empress; she knitted endlessly, and sang lullabies. But socially she was not a success. The transition from princess of an unimportant duchy to the wife of the reigning Emperor of a vast and unfamiliar country was too much for her shy but unyielding temperament. Like her Aunt Vicky in Prussia nearly half a century before, she was shocked by court life – but no warmth of manner helped to soften her disapproval. At official ceremonies Alix stood at her husband's side, awkward and unsmiling. Russian society did nothing to help her: soon they were beginning to speak of her as 'the German Woman'.

Nicholas II

On 25 May, with the year of mourning over, Nicholas made his formal entry into Moscow; the coronation of the new Tsar took place the next day in the Uspensky Cathedral, in a setting of awe-inspiring splendour beneath its five golden cupolas. Nicholas himself placed on his head a nine-pound crown, from which a huge uncut ruby glowed amidst pearls and diamonds. It tended to slip forward over his nose, and its weight made his head ache. He had hoped a lighter crown could be used, but his uncles would not allow any break with tradition. The Empress was crowned with him. While Nicholas flagged, she – who was usually tired by official functions – went through the five-hour ceremony in a state of exaltation. The mysticism of Russian Orthodoxy had taken hold of her: she believed utterly in the Divine anointing of her husband, and felt also that by this ceremony she was being mystically united to Russia.

In the evening, at the Kremlin, a banquet for seven thousand people was followed by a brilliant ball. The less privileged celebrated in the candle-lit streets. Towards dawn thousands of them walked to the Khodynka Meadow, where a traditional open-air feast was to be held for the working people the next day. Some five thousand were there in a cheerful, bawdy mood when the wagons of free beer and souvenir mugs began to arrive at sunrise. Suddenly rumour began, and spread like fire, that there would not be enough beer to go round. The crowd surged forward, the single squadron of Cossacks being quite unable to control them. Disaster followed on a vast scale. Within minutes nearly thirteen hundred people were trampled to death and hundreds more badly injured.

The French Ambassador was giving a ball that evening, and Nicholas's first instinct was not to attend it. But his uncles – not least his uncle Serge who as Governor-General of Moscow was partly responsible for the tragedy – urged his appearance; France was an important ally who must not be offended. Again he gave in to his uncles. They may have been right, but no amount of hospital visiting later could erase from people's minds the callous impression made by his arrival with Alix, both brilliantly dressed, to open the festivities. To the superstitious peasants of Russia, this terrible blot on the brightness of the coronation was an omen of disaster for the new Tsar's reign.

Lenin in 1900

Chapter eight
Fellow Travellers

In 1891 Vladimir Ilyich, younger brother of Alexander Ulyanov who had been hanged for his attempt to blow up Alexander III, arrived in St Petersburg to take his law exams, in which he came first out of a student entry of 124. He was twenty-one. The Director of his school at Simbirsk on the Volga – one Fyodor Kerensky – had noticed in him 'a somewhat excessive tendency toward isolation and reserve', although young Vladimir Ilyich had been an outstanding pupil, coming home regularly with the announcement 'top in everything'. At university he had to behave cautiously because of his close kinship to 'the martyr'; but he read enormously, and Alexander's career was both an inspiration and a warning to him. 'We must find another way,' he said. In 1888 he read Marx's *Das Kapital*. Later he was to adopt, as his revolutionary alias, his elder brother's *nom de guerre* – Lenin.

Within two years of arriving in St Petersburg he was deep in revolutionary work, learning about factory conditions, forming workers' study groups, writing about markets and debating with fellow members of the Russian Social Democratic party. 'Our new Marxist friend treated this question of markets in a very concrete manner,' one of them wrote. 'It was linked up with the interests of the masses, and in the whole approach we sensed . . . live Marxism.'[1] The hard Lenin line had already begun to show. He despised the academic approach of the intellectuals, insisting 'that no advance could be made until the workers themselves were saturated with revolutionary ideas'.[2]

The factory workers of Russia were almost entirely peasants who went to the cities because life on the land was intolerable. They had no rights or protection and were exploited mercilessly, sleeping in crowded dormitories or by their machines and working long hours, under conditions worse than anywhere in Europe, for minute wages. The Russian industrial revolution was built on their backs, and they had neither education nor organisation with which to defend themselves; but they were together and in time they could be united into a militant proletariat. Lenin saw this more clearly than most.

He was already nearly bald, with deep lines on his face. This, with his flattish nose, his slanting eyes, his reddish, neatly-trimmed beard and moustache, his quiet, neat clothes and his contained air of authority, gave him a singular appearance, and made him look older than he was. 'The old man,' they called him in revolutionary circles. He was not a flamboyant orator, but what he said was compelling, packed with knowledge and reason, the sentences thrown out 'like unhewn blocks of granite'. One of his early pupils, a docker, wrote: 'We used to say among ourselves that he had such big brains that they had pushed his hair out.'

On Shrove Tuesday 1893 he met Nadezhda Krupskaya at a secret meeting which was officially a pancake party, and they became close colleagues. Krupskaya, a daughter of impoverished gentlefolk, was a teacher and a fellow-Marxist. She was a quiet, intelligent, motherly young woman with pale skin, broad forehead, intense eyes and a calm and serious manner. She gave classes to workers at the Smolensky Sunday Evening Adult School. Lenin questioned her about them, she brought him news from the workers, and he began to confide in her.

'When we became more closely acquainted, Vladimir Ilyich once told me about the attitude of the Liberals towards the arrest of his elder brother. All acquaintances shunned the Ulyanov family,' she wrote in her memoirs. 'There was no railway at Simbirsk at that time, and Vladimir Ilyich's mother had to go on horseback to Syzran in order to go on to St Petersburg, where her eldest son was imprisoned. Vladimir Ilyich was sent to seek a companion for the journey. But no one wanted to travel with the mother of an arrested man. Vladimir Ilyich told me that this widespread cowardice made a very profound impression on

Nadezhda Krupskaya

him.' It certainly made him uncompromising, if he was not already so by nature. 'The bourgeoisie rules both in life in general and in Liberal society,' he wrote the following year. 'It would seem, therefore, that it is necessary to turn away from this society and go to what is diametrically opposed to the bourgeoisie.' He never changed that opinion.

He visited Paris and discussed the 1871 Commune with Paul Lafargue, Marx's son-in-law, then returned to St Petersburg to found an underground newspaper, *The Workers' Cause,* and worked closely with Julius Martov, the leader of the Marxist Jewish Bund. He laboured unremittingly and was soon the centre of the SD* underground. 'Of all our group Vladimir Ilyich was the best equipped for conspiratorial work. He knew all the through courtyards, and was a skilled hand at giving police-spies the slip. He taught us how to write in books with invisible ink, or by the dot method; how to mark secret signs, and thought out all manner of aliases.'[3]

Lenin was by no means an orthodox Marxist. The Russian SD party had been founded by George Plekhanov, a close associate of Engels. Plekhanov was now a middle-aged father-figure in exile in Geneva, elegant, witty, aloof and doctrinaire. He believed, with Marx, that 'the emancipation of the working class is the work of the working class itself', and based his leadership on a loose amalgamation of independent Marxist groups. Lenin took the opposite view: that only a single, small, loyal, well-trained and utterly determined group could effectively be 'the vanguard of the revolution'; and he held that view, through thick and thin, for the rest of his life.

At the end of 1895 Lenin was arrested, and in January 1897 was sent to Siberia. The following year Krupskaya was exiled, and claimed to be Lenin's fiancée so that they could continue to live and work together. They were married in Siberia that July. Exile under Nicholas II was a lenient affair: Lenin lived in peace and reasonable comfort in a quiet village, hunted and skated, and, with Krupskaya's help, translated Sidney and Beatrice Webb's *History of Trade Unionism.* It was probably the happiest part of his life.

On his release in 1900, he went to Europe, where Krupskaya found him a year later in a small, badly furnished room in

* The Russian Social Democratic Party.

Munich, drinking tea 'out of a tin mug which he himself washed thoroughly and hung up on a nail by the tap'.[4] In the spring of 1902 they moved to London and rented two rooms at 30 Holford Square in the names of Dr and Mrs Richter; the landlady thought they were German and hoped they were properly married. No one interfered with them and Lenin started editing a new revolutionary paper – *Iskra,* 'The Spark' – which was smuggled into Russia and became the centre of a powerful cell of SD exiles which included Martov and was joined by Trotsky – who arrived one night, an unexpected stranger, from Siberia.

Lev Bronstein – 'the young eagle', 'the greatest Jew since Christ'[5] – borrowed his revolutionary name of Trotsky from a warder when hurriedly forging a passport. He had been arrested in Odessa as a revolutionary, and escaped after four years; he was still only twenty-three. 'He had a wonderfully quiet mind and a rich, deep voice. With his broad chest, his huge forehead, surmounted by great masses of black, waving hair, his strong, fierce eyes, and his heavy protruding lips, he is the very incarnation of the revolutionary of the bourgeois caricatures.'[6] Lenin was amazed by his fervour and brilliance, and they immediately embarked on a revolutionary dialogue which was to last, on and off, for more than twenty years.

Lenin also recommended him to Plekhanov as a member of the controlling board which was to organise the next party Congress; but Plekhanov did not share Lenin's enthusiasm for Trotsky, and rejected this idea along with many others that came from London. A showdown between Lenin and Plekhanov was clearly due.

The Congress was held in the summer of 1903. The strain of its preparation made Lenin ill, but he recovered in time to attend and dominate it. More than fifty delegates, representing different Russian groups, met in Brussels for what was intended to be a secret conference, but the chances of keeping the meeting of over fifty excited Russians secret were negligible: they could be heard three blocks away, and one of them sang arias in the evenings loudly enough to draw crowds outside their hotel. After nine sessions the Belgian police moved them on, and the Congress was reconvened in London, in a red-draped hall off Tottenham Court Road – perhaps not far from the original home of Franz Josef's furniture.

Although Plekhanov took the chair, Lenin had nominated

Trotsky

118

most of the delegates and prepared the order of business. First the Jewish Bund and the Economists were thrown out; both were independent Marxist groups which objected to Lenin's 'Jacobin-like' policy of a dictatorial central power, but Lenin prevailed. Even Martov – a gentle, rather nervous man – was alienated, and when the basic rules were debated he opposed Lenin's call for a revolutionary *élite* which would, as Trotsky put it, form 'a dictatorship over the proletariat'. Martov won, but only with the help of the Jewish Bund's and Economists' votes; when they ceded, his following became the minority – *mensheviki* in Russian – and Lenin's the majority – *bolsheviki*. It was brilliantly and ruthlessly done; Lenin emerged as the head of virtually a new party within the SD movement, though at the price of total isolation from the other leaders. Martov accused him of 'Bonapartism of the worst type', and even Trotsky was shocked and joined the Mensheviks. Lenin fell ill again and went off to recuperate in Switzerland, without friends; but Bolshevism had been born.

In Russia, the tradition of the *Narodnaya Volya* lived on and became formally the SR Party* in 1901. The following year it formed an inner, secret Terrorist Brigade, for the sole purpose of assassination. The SRs were not inspired by Marxist theory: their actions arose out of a spontaneous and entirely Russian sense of revolt, and their Terrorist Brigade consisted of dedicated and doomed individuals, infiltrated by a fair sprinkling of spies from the Tsarist secret police, the *Okhrana*. In 1903 a police spy, Azev, actually became head of the Brigade.

Azev, a toad-like young man of unusual astuteness, had paid for his education by becoming a butter salesman, selling a consignment privately and absconding with the proceeds to Germany, where he became a student at Karlsruhe Polytechnic. He was soon working for a group of revolutionary *émigrés* but, running out of funds, wrote to the *Okhrana,* sending details of the group's activities and offering his services for a regular fee of fifty roubles a month. The *Okhrana* enrolled him as an *agent provocateur*. An inspired organiser, he rose rapidly and silently to the top of the SR movement, made a great deal of money and

* Russian Social Revolutionary Party, commonly known as Socialist Revolutionaries.

became one of the most successful double agents in history. The police knew him as Valentine and valued him highly, but he told them only what he wanted them to know, and protected those terrorists who were useful to him. His list of prospective targets was impressive and included Vyacheslav Plehve (the Minister of the Interior), Grand Duke Serge, and the Tsar himself.

Apart from the Terrorist Brigade, the Socialist Revolutionaries had many more moderate followers among the intelligentsia and mass support from the peasantry. In fact their doctrines, such as they were, were founded on an idealised regard for peasant-based, Christian Russian society. The most notable of them, Alexander Kerensky, became Lenin's chief opponent in the Revolution.

Kerensky was an orator, a passionate humanist, enthusiastic, able, brilliant in debate, theatrical, egotistical, and convinced that Russia's spirit and destiny were linked with his own. By one of those preposterous coincidences which read so improbably in Russian novels, Kerensky was born and brought up in the same small town as Lenin, and his father was the Director of Education who had observed Lenin at school. Kerensky also went to St Petersburg to read law. He was eleven years younger than Lenin, but he knew the family and wrote long afterwards:

Let no one say that Lenin is an expression of some kind of allegedly Asiatic 'elemental Russian force'. I was born under the same sky, I breathed the same air, I heard the same peasant songs and played in the same college playground. I saw the same limitless horizons from the same high bank of the Volga and I know in my blood and bones – that it is only by losing all touch with our native land, only by stamping out all native feeling for it, only so could one do what Lenin did in deliberately and cruelly mutilating Russia.[7]

In St Petersburg, from 1899 on, Kerensky was a member of a student circle with a mildly Socialist Revolutionary point of view. His own preferences were legalistic and parliamentary: he chose to be a barrister, dedicating his career to the defence of political prisoners and victims of the *Okhrana* in court-rooms all over the country. He toyed with the idea of joining the Liberals, but Russian liberals were as much wedded to the concept of constitutional monarchy as those of other countries; they only hoped to persuade the Tsar into some reasonable modification of

Alexander Kerensky

autocracy. It was the behaviour of the Tsar himself which turned Kerensky away. To him Nicholas II was a worse autocrat than Alexander III, whose edicts had at least conformed to established law, 'but Nicholas II completely ignored it, in the belief that his will, no matter how much it went against the laws in force, was binding on all his subjects. . . . It was this that now led me to the inescapable conclusion that for the salvation of Russia and her future the reigning monarch must be removed.'[8]

Compared with those in Austria and even Germany, the liberal movement in Russia was tiny and weak, but in these years it began to gather itself together. It had two precarious strongholds, one in the universities, the other in the *zemstva*. Russian liberals tended, therefore, to be either university intellectuals or enlightened country gentlemen, of which there were few. By far the most important figure among them was Paul Milyukov. Born on the same day as Wilhelm II, 27 January 1859, he studied history at Moscow University under the great Klyuchevsky. Milyukov grew up a liberal, and himself succeeded to the chair of history at Moscow.

Since 1868 student unrest had been dealt with summarily, but the very exertion of repression forced it into new outbreaks in which the more progressive members of the staff were compromised. In 1896 a University demonstration in Moscow was suppressed by the police, and Milyukov dismissed from his post and exiled from the city for ten years. In the same year the police also crushed a meeting of *zemstvo* chairmen, who had hoped to set up a national congress. But demonstrations continued, and in the following year a student called Vera Vetrova burnt herself to death in front of the Peter-Paul fortress at St Petersburg in protest against the régime.

Milyukov travelled about, publishing illegal liberal journals, and was twice arrested, but in July 1903 he helped to found the Union of Liberation – a coalition, rather than a party, of groups with similar aims, dominated by liberals and *zemstvo* leaders. From then on, Milyukov was its main spokesman. 'A fine scholar and a man of high personal integrity, somewhat cold in temperament and without charm and lustre in his relations with other men,' is how a later historian describes him. 'From first to last his liberalism was derived from western thought and

Count Sergius Witte

was in almost every respect discordant with Russian experience and tradition.'[9] All the same, he was a force to be reckoned with.

To the extreme right of this parade of reformers stood Sergius Witte; as Minister of Finance, he was the only one of them to have the ear of the Tsar. Witte had risen from the post of traffic manager of the south-western railway to be Alexander III's Minister of Communications, and was the only apparent influence of enlightenment on the old Tsar or the new. 'I made several attempts to draw His Majesty's attention to the peasant problem,' he complained. 'But my efforts were constantly thwarted.' Although an insufferable and arrogant man, and no radical, Witte had a good administrative brain and achieved immense material benefits for his country. He was responsible for the building of the Trans-Siberian railway, the inflow of overseas capital for industrialisation, and much good sense in foreign affairs. He was a cynic, a bully and of no certain party; but he at least saw that, without some social reform, the whole industrial fabric of the new Russia, of which he was the chief architect, was in danger of collapse.

Witte carried almost unrivalled weight at the Imperial Council, and used it to attempt some modernising of society; yet even he made no progress with the Tsar, who alternately trusted and disliked him but never did anything. Witte's failure to move the body politic forward was perhaps fatal, and his final indictment of Nicholas is as monumental as any. 'His character is the source of all our misfortunes,' he wrote. 'He is incapable of steering the Ship of State into a quiet harbour. His outstanding failure is a lamentable lack of will power. Though benevolent and not unintelligent, this short-coming disqualifies him totally as the unlimited autocratic ruler of the Russian people.'

Chapter nine
The Years of Blood

Europe's historic capitals had begun to wear a sooty look; trams clanged through them, and smoke from factory chimneys darkened the formal buildings at their hearts. There was much inequality and poverty even in the richest countries, though not on the Russian scale; but this worried their rulers less than suspicion and fear of each other.

The political cornerstone of Central Europe was still Bismarck's old alliance, the Triple Entente between Germany, Austria and Italy, which now faced the new Dual Entente between Russia and France. Britain remained neutral in the European power-game and preoccupied by her Empire. Only Kaiser Wilhelm seemed interested in wooing her, and that in a capricious and condescending way.

When Queen Victoria was dying in January 1901, Wilhelm hurried to Osborne and, elbowing his way between her English relations, held her in his arms while she died. He had always genuinely loved her, and he insisted on staying for the funeral and behaved so 'nicely' that his Uncle Bertie, now King Edward VII, made him a Field Marshal; but their mutual antipathy remained.

Wilhelm had mellowed a little with power: he was a happy-seeming, if irritable, Kaiser, roaring with laughter, travelling incessantly, intervening in everything, and taking his favourite ministers on yachting trips in the Baltic, where they were forced to do imitations and physical jerks and allow themselves to be

Wilhelm II follows Edward VII in Queen Victoria's funeral procession

playfully pushed over from behind by their Imperial master. Among his other enthusiasms Wilhelm was in love with the sea, and with naval uniforms and navies. His ambition, which had alarmed Bismarck, was to be arbiter not only of European but of world affairs, and although his motives were as much benevolent as arrogant, his methods soon brought him into conflict with his potential English allies. In a way it was a conflict he welcomed:

his pride demanded that he should appear as strong as they. 'I am not in a position to go beyond the strictest neutrality and I must first get for myself a fleet,' he said in 1900, and immediately launched a twenty-year building programme to create a German Navy powerful enough to face the British fleet in the North Sea.

As Britain only felt safe with a navy at least as big as any two others, Edward and his government were alarmed and offended, and since Wilhelm's 'soft' attitude to Britain was not shared by his ministers, tension between the two countries grew. In October 1901 Joseph Chamberlain told a German envoy, 'There can be no further question of association between England and Germany'. The British government looked in other directions, and made a pact with Japan. In the same year Vicky died, painfully, of cancer of the spine, at the age of sixty. Wilhelm's closest links with England had gone. Left more or less alone in Europe, and uneasily placed between France and Russia, he turned his attention to Nicky. His conceptual ideas were always bold and often shrewd; it was his execution of them that was ludicrous. It seemed to him, and to his ministers, that the best way to neutralise Russia was to turn her attention to the east, and to that end he began to bombard Nicholas with exhortations to fulfil his 'Holy Mission' in Asia. 'It is the great task of the future for Russia to cultivate the Asian continent and to defend Europe from the Great Yellow Race,' he wrote, and sent Nicky several large, allegorical pictures, painted to his own execrable design, of the Tsar in armour, supported by a towering Kaiser, fighting off the Yellow Peril – which, incidentally, Wilhelm genuinely feared.

The Romanovs laughed a good deal. Both Alexandra and the Dowager Empress Marie disliked Wilhelm, but Nicholas had a sneaking regard for him, and the notion of a far-eastern crusade suited the Tsar's plans rather well. For several years Russian forces had been picking bits off China and Manchuria and had browbeaten Japan into handing over Port Arthur, which gave Russia a far-eastern port and naval base at the end of Witte's new Trans-Siberian railway. Siberia itself was gradually being developed, as part of Witte's economic strategy, and a good many would-be millionaires at the Tsarist court had financial stakes in Russian expansion eastwards at Japan's expense. The pressures upon Nicholas to push his luck against the Japanese began to mount.

One of these pressures was the state of affairs at home. In 1902

Vyacheslav Plehve inherited the Ministry of the Interior from Sipyagin who had been assassinated by the SR terrorists, and brought with him an era of police repression which soon achieved world-wide notoriety. The *Okhrana* was reinforced, censorship extended, liberals and revolutionaries persecuted equally, and national minorities – particularly Jews – oppressed. In one town, at Easter 1903, nearly fifty Jews were murdered and six hundred Jewish homes destroyed. Witte warned Plehve, 'If you go on like this you will be assassinated yourself'; but Plehve relied upon Azev to keep the Terrorist Brigade away from him.

Nicholas spent most of his time at Tsarskoe Selo, in the complex of palaces which Catherine the Great had built for herself sixteen miles outside St Petersburg. In this heavily guarded enclosure of unreality he worked assiduously and ineptly as Head of State, and lived a rather anglicised private life with his wife and four young daughters. In ten years of marriage Alix had developed into a devoted wife and mother, but she was plagued by rheumatism and had failed to produce a son in spite of at least one hysterical false pregnancy. She was now pregnant again. Increasingly neurotic, she felt passionately Russian and was fascinated by the mysticism of the Orthodox Church. Nicholas's religious sense was more superficial, but sincere enough, and he was deeply fatalistic. It seemed to him, as it did to Franz Josef, that if he was born for trouble he could not avoid it, but must continue to do his best to uphold the traditions of Divine Right which had been thrust upon him. Since any kind of reform was an encroachment on that right, he refused even to consider it, but relied on Plehve's reign of terror and hoped for better days.

As hatred of Plehve, and of the Tsar himself and his whole administration, spread through the country, strikes broke out and culminated in a general strike in July 1903. The strike was broken and Plehve, who was one of the anti-Japan faction, suggested 'a small victorious war to stem the tide of revolution'. When Witte objected, Nicholas relieved him of his Ministry and continued to provoke Japan. The Japanese reacted by attacking Port Arthur and sinking a large part of the Russian Far East Fleet in the early spring of 1904.

No one, at least in Russia, believed that a small oriental state could defeat the Tsarist empire; but Russian incompetence, the remoteness of the battlefield and the suicidal determination of the Japanese produced a holocaust which shook Russia to the roots for the next two years. Having gained command of the sea, Japan was able to land and supply her entire army in Manchuria, where it forced the Russian troops northwards in a succession of enormous and bloody battles, leaving the Russian garrison in Port Arthur isolated. The Russians seem to have fought with great bravery at first under inept and contradictory orders, short of supplies, comfort or quick reinforcement; but isolated in the Manchurian wastes, at the mercy of a better-armed and fanatical enemy, their morale and numbers gradually dwindled. By the end of a few months Russia had lost over a hundred thousand men in conditions of appalling hardship.

Nicholas ordered the Baltic Fleet out of Kronstadt to sail around the world to the North China Sea, and more men and supplies were dispatched eastwards along the Trans-Siberian railway. What little enthusiasm there had been for the war disappeared as the cost in men and food and fuel made itself felt, and by the middle of the year apathy had turned again to unrest. In July Azev's men moved in on Plehve.

Plehve was on his way to an audience with the Tsar when an SR terrorist group threw into his coach a bomb which blew him into several pieces, to the delight and relief of almost everyone in Russia except the Romanovs and their most conservative supporters. Nicholas's reaction – 'I have a secret conviction that I am destined for a terrible trial' – was a characteristically self-centred but accurate prophecy: one can almost hear, behind the words, the dreaded footfall of anarchy approaching the Imperial nursery. Two days afterwards, he was consoled by the birth of his long-awaited heir, but a week later news of another disaster reached him: the remnants of the Russian Far East Fleet, venturing out of besieged Port Arthur, were scattered by the Japanese, and the commander killed in his bombarded flagship, the *Tsarevich*. It was an oddly symbolic coincidence: within a few weeks it was known – though only by Nicholas and Alix and their doctors – that the infant Tsarevich Alexis was suffering from his own affliction of the blood. His haemophilia, an exclusively male complaint, inherited through his mother and Queen Victoria, left his life and the succession of the monarchy constantly in doubt, adding another strand of torture to the cords already being drawn around this self-doomed family.

The falling fortunes of its government left Russia with the three classic alternatives, of repression, revolution, or liberal constitutional compromise, and from them history made its irrevocable choice. If, during the following months, revolution had succeeded, or if liberal moderation had prevailed, our present-day political world would be unrecognisably different; but the revolutionaries were not ready, and the liberals saw their chance and bungled it.

In autumn 1904 Russian liberals' hopes were high, but their numbers were small and they felt in need of allies. In October Milyukov, now their unchallenged leader, attended a conference of almost all Russian radical and revolutionary parties, and emerged from it an ally of the revolutionaries. The logic on both sides was tortuous and faulty. Milyukov's narrow and uncompromising aim was an immediate, fully-fledged Western-style constitution, such as had been the ambition of liberal Europeans from the Prince Consort onwards: he had inherited an 'English weakness' as fatal as the Tsarevich's. What made him believe that the gentle plant of constitutional liberalism, which had withered in more promising soil, could spring fully-flowered from the unbroken political ground of Russia is not clear; but he did believe it, and most liberals followed him.

Most of the revolutionaries also believed it. Marx had always assumed that liberalism would overthrow autocracy and that only after that, in the comparative freedom of a bourgeois society, would socialism be able to grow and eventually take over. Therefore it seemed logical to everyone concerned that, however different their ultimate goals, liberals and revolutionary socialists should combine for the time being against a shaken Tsar and force instant parliamentary rule upon Russia.

Shrewd conservatives, like Bismarck in Germany, had long foreseen the outcome of such a combination, and Milyukov would have done better to remember the words of that old Austrian arch-reactionary, Metternich, nearly a century before: 'Liberalism is but the accomplice of demagogy and serves, very often unconsciously, to drive a road for it and often to level it most conveniently. Liberalism shares the fate of all forerunners. Once the true leader appears, it is almost impossible to find any traces of the forerunner. Nothing is further from liberalism than demagogy; this latter is categorical, tyrannical in its ends as in its choice of means.'

St Petersburg in winter was a frozen city, divided by a frozen river, and the flat country around it desolate with ice and snow. To the north, the cold sea stretched away to Finland, which was then a Russian province. At the mouth of the River Neva the Peter and Paul Fortress stood guard, its spire shining above the rooftops, and along the southern bank of the river were ranged the Winter Palace, the government buildings and the great houses of the rich, the Nevsky Prospekt opening between them. Bridges led to the other bank where the main mass of workers lived in narrower streets and in tenements around the dark satanic mills of the Vyborg district, cold and undernourished and unprivileged, but organised now in trade unions, some of them run, as well as infiltrated, by the secret police.

As news of violence in Russia and defeats in Manchuria entered the city, this mass stirred. Demonstrators flowed over the bridges into the Nevsky Prospekt, but transiently, with a sort of aimless discontent; and in the enormous Putilov steel-works a strike began, born of weariness. Then, in the first days of 1905, Port Arthur fell to the Japanese, and the shock of this distant catastrophe stung the city into life.

The march which followed on Bloody Sunday was not directly inspired by the Social Democrats or Socialist Revolutionaries, who still had no effective leadership inside Russia, but was a spontaneous outburst of despair, and Father Gapon, who led it, a confused and histrionic puppet. A young ex-prison chaplain, an orator, with a messianic but unschooled devotion to the people's cause, Gapon was the *Okhrana's* odd choice as head of the Association of Russian Factory and Mill Workers, one of the 'police unions' through which the government hoped subtly to influence and control its work-force. When pushed forward by the rank and file of workers, he was glad enough to turn his back on his police connections and lead a multitude with a humble petition direct to the Tsar, asking 'for ending of the war, for full civil liberties, and political amnesty and a constituent assembly',[1] and anything else that came into their heads.

Some hundred and twenty thousand men, women and children turned out that January Sunday, bare-headed in the cold, carrying church banners and ikons and the Tsar's portrait, and singing hymns and the Imperial anthem, 'God Save the Tsar'. They converged in separate processions towards the Winter Palace. But Nicholas had left the city, for safety, and they were met by

Bloody Sunday, 22 January 1905. Father Gapon and his followers are met by troops

charges of cossacks and dragoons. Several hundred were killed and the story went round a disapproving world. In England Ramsay Macdonald called the Tsar a 'blood-stained creature' and a 'common murderer'. Kerensky, who witnessed it, sent a letter of protest to the officers of the regiments concerned, and Gapon wrote a frantic denunciation of Nicholas and then fled the country. More than any other single event, Bloody Sunday opened the eyes of the Russian public to the weakness not only of the Tsarist administration but of the Tsar himself. The wretched Nicholas noted in his diary: 'a painful day'.

More painful ones followed. Strikes, demonstrations and terrorist attacks spread across the country. In Moscow in the middle of February Azev's SR terrorists destroyed the Grand Duke Serge at the gates of the Kremlin. (Serge was probably the most hated man in Russia after Plehve. He was Nicholas's uncle and the husband of Alix's sister Ella: the terror was coming near home.) A week later the main Russian army was routed in

Bloody Sunday

Manchuria with enormous losses, and the next month the peasants rose and began to pillage and burn landlords' estates. Milyukov and the liberals and the *zemstva* themselves joined in the general demand for reform, allied now with the Socialist Revolutionaries. In May the Russian Baltic Fleet finally arrived in the China seas and was immediately sunk by the Japanese; the following month the sailors of the battleship *Potemkin* led a mutiny of the Black Sea Fleet. Nicholas, in despair, sent Witte to America to negotiate peace with Japan.

Meanwhile Gapon had arrived in Switzerland and met Lenin and Trotsky, who were now more or less reconciled although Trotsky was still a Menshevik. Trotsky decided to return at once to Russia with another SD exile, Parvus; but Lenin thought the time not yet ripe for revolution. Gapon, however, followed Trotsky and joined the Socialist Revolutionaries, although he also – as a piece of personal insurance – renewed his contact with the *Okhrana*.

Out of this seething uproar a general strike developed and paralysed Russia. Even the liberal unions, even the Imperial ballet company, even Nicholas's former mistress Kschessinska, joined it. In St Petersburg a workers' soviet, which included Trotsky and Parvus, took over the city, and the Imperial family were trapped in the Peterhof Palace out on the Gulf of Finland and accessible only by sea. Lenin, thinking that he had been wrong, travelled to Sweden, where he waited for a forged passport to take him home. Even Kerensky offered his services to the SR Terrorist Brigade, who rejected them – Kerensky was not the stuff of which terrorists are made.

In the middle of all this Witte returned with remarkably moderate peace terms from Japan and the prospect of an enormous new loan from France to put Russia on her feet again. Nicholas made him a Count and Chief Minister. To Nicholas and most Russians he was the only effective minister left: suddenly he was the man of the hour.

When Witte insisted on the creation of some kind of constitution, Nicholas had no other option although, as he confessed to his mother, he felt sick with shame at this betrayal of the dynasty. Had the revolt been restricted to the towns, Tsarist absolutism need not have been at stake; but when the peasants rose as well the whole dynastic basis of Imperial Russia was shaken. After much agonised argument, an Imperial Manifesto, prepared by Witte, was issued by Nicholas in October 1905. It promised freedom of the individual and the creation of a State Duma, with limited but considerable power, to be elected by the different classes of society, though not on a one-man-one-vote system: for all its shortcomings, a form of parliament. It was not enough for the revolutionaries. 'The people', Trotsky wrote in *Izvestia*, 'rejects the police whip wrapped in the parchment of the constitution.' But it might have been enough for the liberals had not Milyukov been so fatally committed to the slogan of instant constitutional democracy. 'Nothing has changed,' he declared. 'The struggle goes on.'

One can understand the liberals' reluctance to be associated with an imperfect parliament in what was still a police state, and they knew too that the Tsar's heart was not in the reforms; but at least it was a possible beginning of better things, and they were the only people who could make it work. When Witte offered them seats in his Ministry, he needed them as much as they needed him. He was talented in the art of the possible, and reckoned that with full liberal support he could carry the new legislation through.

They rejected him, and so caused his downfall and ultimately their own. Isolated, Witte twisted and turned, hated by left and right, and national unrest continued. Trotsky took over the St Petersburg soviet and called another general strike; the sailors at Kronstadt mutinied; troops were sent out to put down resistance in the cities and the countryside; other troops, returning disgruntled and dangerous from Manchuria, were shot; even Kerensky was arrested. Lenin, home at last, went with Krupskaya and Gapon to Moscow to support the Moscow soviet's stand against the Semenovsky regiment. After ten days of fighting and artillery bombardment, the Moscow workers gave in: as Delescluze had found in Paris in 1871, hand arms at barricades are no match for fully armed troops. Lenin learnt that lesson, although he did still think the revolution could succeed. Meanwhile he, Krupskaya and Gapon fled to Finland, where Gapon was later found and hanged as a traitor by Azev's SR terrorists. The St Petersburg soviet collapsed and Trotsky was sent back to Siberia, but escaped on the way. The edge of rebellion was blunted.

Nicholas breathed again, and dispensed with Witte. As soon as the French loan was negotiated, Witte resigned and his place was taken by court reactionaries. The promises of the October Manifesto were curtailed, and by the time the first State Duma was elected its powers had become negligible. The liberals, realising their mistake, renounced the revolution and agreed to sit in the now emasculated Duma; but they were too late – their moment of opportunity had passed. Despised by the socialist parties (who boycotted the First Duma entirely), hated by the conservatives, and distrusted by the Tsar, they were without friends; although they fought on bravely and honourably for liberty and democracy, they never again had any real prospect of governing Russia.

Nicholas, too, had thrown off his only lifeline. For the moment, Tsarism was back in the saddle and using the whip; but at its heart now there was nothing more than a discredited, anxious little man with a neurotic wife and a haemophiliac son.

Chapter ten

Uncle Bertie and the Bear

At the other end of Europe, in Britain, liberalism was doing rather better, and so was the monarch. The brash, acquisitive imperialism of the nineteenth century, which had led to the Boer War and many other punitive expeditions, had given way to a mellower enjoyment of the fruits of empire.

Lenin and his fellow-communists were unharassed in early twentieth-century London, and in 1905 a liberal government with a radical wing came into office, while a popular song declared:

> There won't be no war,
> Not while we've got a king
> Like Good King Edward,
> 'Cos he hates that sort of thing.

Edward's attitude to politics, as to other things, was patrician but permissive: on principle he objected to the radicalism of Lloyd George and Winston Churchill and to indiscretion in society, though in fact he tolerated the one and was guilty of the other. After years of uncompromising Victorianism, the British were glad to have an easy-going, naughty King. He was certainly preferable to Kaiser Wilhelm, both at home and abroad. As his private secretary wrote, 'Our King makes a better show than William. He has more graciousness and dignity. William is ungracious, nervous and plain.'

Edward VII and Queen Alexandra

Edward was sixty when he came to the throne, and had survived almost a lifetime of parental disapproval. Indolent and profligate, he had been the despair of his mother, whom in some ways he resembled: he was sensible and sympathetic and he improved with age. As his sexual agility declined, his personal relationships stabilised. He settled into an equable relationship with Alice Keppel, and his wife Alexandra – the beautiful Danish sister of the Dowager Empress Marie of Russia – made a tolerant, decorative and popular Queen. The sun shone on Edwardian England.

Gross, gutteral, bronchial and touchy, old Edward was a charmer all the same, and surprisingly conscientious, once the duties of kingship were his. He got muddled sometimes, and once handed the Kaiser his own confidential briefing notes for their meeting; but he understood exactly the role of a constitutional sovereign, and although his intellectual grasp was none too firm, he was a natural diplomatist and knew how to take advice. Within a few years he was the senior diplomat of Europe.

Britain and France, the only tolerably democratic powers in Europe, faced the three huge, absolute monarchies of Austria, Germany and Russia, and of those three Germany was the most potent and frightening. In Germany Wilhelm's credit with his own ministers was falling, but he still spoke grandly and intemperately for his nation, and as often as possible at Britain's expense. His extraordinarily ambivalent attitude to England became more evident as he grew more and more dangerously erratic. In England he talked about blood being thicker than water and of securing European peace by the combined might of the German army and the British navy; while at home he spoke of 'a war between us and England in which we are driven to attack France', and dismissed the British cabinet as 'noodles'. 'What', Edward wondered, 'would the Kaiser say if I called his Ministers such nice names?'

At the beginning of his reign, Edward had considerable hopes of an Anglo–German *entente*. The British mistrusted Russia and were on bad terms with France, and Wilhelm had spoken of the benefits of an alliance between the 'two teutonic nations'; but the implacable hostility of the German government and Wilhelm's behaviour combined to make that impossible. Personally Edward and Wilhelm had always disliked each other. Wilhelm

Edward VII in 1902 with his grandchildren, Edward, Henry, Mary and Albert

called his uncle 'a Satan' and 'the arch-intriguer and mischief-maker in Europe', while Edward referred to his nephew as 'the most brilliant failure in history'. All the same, Edward did his best to keep up appearances, giving and receiving visits, although he never felt comfortable in Wilhelm's palaces, where his liberal attitude to politics and sex was disapproved of and he was not allowed to smoke.

Inevitably Britain and France drew closer together, and after Edward's triumphantly successful visit to Paris in 1903 an agreement was signed between the two countries – the *entente cordiale.* In view of France's understanding with Russia, Britain was now committed to Europe, and in June 1908 Edward set sail in the royal yacht *Victoria and Albert,* accompanied by an admiral, a general, senior Foreign Office officials and his marine painter-in-ordinary, to meet the Russian Imperial family in the Baltic, off Reval. 'King Edward did not patronise the Tsar – he treated him as a highly successful nephew.'[1] The Tsar's entourage were in his own yachts, the *Standart* and the *Polaris,* and festivities spread across the three vessels. There was feasting and dancing, Edward put on his uniform of the Kiev Dragoons, the bands played *The Merry Widow* and the painter painted. Nicholas was cheerful and relaxed, Alix smiled, old memories of happy days at Coburg and Windsor were revived and a good time was had by all.

It was the apotheosis of Edwardian diplomacy. Nicholas was accompanied by his new Chief Minister, Peter Stolypin, and his Foreign Minister, Izvolsky, and while the royals exchanged family gossip and took photographs of each other, the first moves were made towards an understanding between Britain, Russia and France. From that year onwards Europe was critically divided between the central powers, Germany and Austria-Hungary, on the one hand and the new *triple entente* on the other. Winston Churchill, then a junior minister serving his first term, wrote, 'It was the first step towards Armageddon!'

Edward, however, continued his amiable tours of the continent. Every year he went to Marienbad in Austria to take the cure, together with his Prime Minister, Sir Henry Campbell-Bannerman, who had turned out to be a congenial club-man; and from there he often went on to visit the Austrian Emperor, whom he also liked. Franz Josef was a lonely old man: the Empress Elizabeth had been stabbed to death by an Italian anarchist at Geneva in 1898; his brother and his son were dead; and he was hardly on speaking terms with his current heir, the Archduke Franz Ferdinand. Edward joined the Emperor at his country home at Bad Ischl and took him for his first and only drive in a motor-car: Franz Josef disliked modern inventions like cars, typewriters and telephones, and would have no truck with any of them. He was more hidebound and cautious than

Franz Josef   *Franz Ferdinand*

ever. When Edward left Ischl in August 1908 they were, as usual, on the best of terms, but Franz Josef had said nothing of a little act of aggression which his government had in mind.

When Bismarck fell, a quarter of a century before, Franz Josef had remarked enviously, 'I wish I had him'. As it was, he was less satisfactorily served. The Dual Monarchy, far from healing the wounds of the minorities within the Empire, had left them to fester, and after Rudolf's death they had no possible doctor in Vienna. By 1908 the condition of the Balkans had become acute. As the Turkish empire withdrew from Europe, the Slav inhabitants of the Balkans demanded their independence and looked to Russia, the great Slav power, for support. Serbia was already independent, but its two neighbouring states, Bosnia and Herzegovena (they are all regions of Yugoslavia now), were administered by Austria, and Franz Josef's government wanted to absorb them completely into the Austrian empire to prevent them from going the way of Serbia. As this was forbidden by

international treaty, and in any case likely to provoke resistance from Russia, Franz Josef had every reason to keep quiet about it; but both the head of the Austrian army, Field Marshal Conrad von Hötzendorff, and the Foreign Minister, von Aehrenthal, were determined to take the risk. In September 1908 Aehrenthal and Izvolsky, the Russian Foreign Minister, met privately in the castle of Buchlau, north of Vienna.

Izvolsky had taken office in 1906, with Stolypin, and was directly answerable to him. It was a conservative ministry, but a not untalented one. Peter Stolypin, a large, bear-like man of stolid courage and vigorous patriotism, was probably the biggest piece of luck ever to come Nicholas's way. As Governor of Saratov province during the 1905 rebellion he had established a reputation for firmness and fairness, and he was brought to St Petersburg in 1906 when Witte fell, and first made Minister of the Interior and then President of the Council of Ministers. After a year of parliamentary chaos he emerged as the strong man of Russia: within that time he had swung the electoral system to the right, initiated a violent purge of the remaining revolutionaries, and announced a system of land reform. There was no doubting his conservatism, but he did believe in a very gradual progress towards constitutional monarchy, once law and order were re-established, and he managed to carry the Tsar with him. 'The more I see of that man,' Nicholas declared, 'the more I like him.'

Stolypin's determination to reimpose the government's authority led to a series of trials and executions which sickened even the moderate left, and Kerensky went from court-room to court-room defending the victims with a success on which he built a nationwide reputation as the advocate of freedom; but Stolypin's will prevailed and produced a new mood in Russia. Under him Russians turned their backs on the losses and humiliation of the Japanese war and the divisions of the 1905 revolution. 'We want a great Russia,' Stolypin told them, and it looked as if they might even achieve it. His rural reforms created a new class of landowning yeoman farmers – 'the sober and the strong' – from among the more enterprising peasantry. These were the *kulaks*: by 1914 there were nearly ten million of them, and their contribution was to make the countryside more loyal

Peter Stolypin

and more productive. On this firm base the cities could be supplied, industry increased, and both prosperity and armed power rebuilt; but it was a long haul.

The wealth and power of western Europe far exceeded Russia's, and in military strength Germany stood head and shoulders above everyone else, restless and menacing. The Tsar's government knew that, however hard they worked, Russia would not be fit to risk a European war before 1917 at the earliest, and Stolypin's foreign policy was supposed to be based on that. But Izvolsky had other ideas.

Izvolsky was a representative diplomat of his age: elegant, resourceful, shifty, a little old-fashioned. For him the traditional goal of Russian foreign policy, the removal of the Turks from the Dardanelles, was more important than the desperate present need of peace in the Balkans. If Austria, backed by Germany, moved into the Balkans, Russia would be faced with a challenge which she dare not meet; but Izvolsky, like the Austrians, was prepared to take a risk.

When Izvolsky met Aehrenthal at Buchlau in September 1908, they made a deal: Austria would allow Russia the freedom of the Dardanelles, and in return Russia would condone Austria's annexation of Bosnia. The two acts of aggression would occur simultaneously, so that the world would be presented with an agreed *fait accompli* which it was sure to accept. For some insane reason the Russian Foreign Minister committed the deal to paper, and the paper went into the Austrian Foreign Minister's pocket. Aehrenthal was a colder and cleverer man than Izvolsky.

Three weeks later, Austria annexed Bosnia without warning. Izvolsky begged Stolypin to take the Dardanelles, but Stolypin refused to move without the agreement of the other European powers. Izvolsky hurried round Europe with his guilty secret, trying to drum up support, but failed. Meanwhile Serbia, on behalf of the Balkan Slavs, appealed to the Tsar to help throw the Austrians out of Bosnia, but the Russians dared not act. In addition to the danger of blackmail by Aehrenthal, there was the greater fear that, if it came to fighting, the Germans would support Austria, under the terms of Bismarck's treaty of 1879. Bismarck had not specifically committed Germany to follow Austria into an adventure in the Balkans unless it suited her – he saw too clearly what the results could be – but the treaty provided the excuse for it, and Wilhelm and his ministers were less

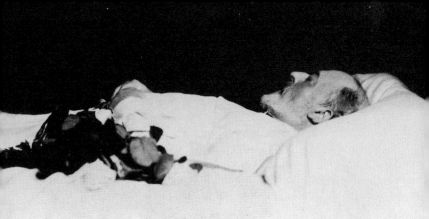

Edward VII after death

given to caution. Indeed, they needed to bind Austria into an armed alliance in case they soon had to face a war with France and Russia simultaneously. So Wilhelm proclaimed himself to Franz Josef as 'a knight in shining armour' standing beside him, and the German Chief-of-Staff assured his opposite number in Austria, von Hötzendorff, 'The moment Russia mobilises, Germany . . . will unquestionably mobilise her whole army'.

In the face of this threat, Russia had to withdraw its support from Serbia, a deep humiliation for the great pan-Slav state. Early in 1909 Nicholas wrote, 'German action towards us has been simply brutal and we won't forget it'. From then on the army in South-west Russia was kept at instant readiness, and Izvolsky, after painful confessions to Stolypin and the Tsar, remained in exile as Russian ambassador to Paris. Aehrenthal – cool, calculating, aloof and dying of cancer – made no effort to soften the blow either to the Slavs or to Izvolsky. 'Aehrenthal is the devil incarnate,' Edward VII complained, but he could do nothing. The lines of battle had been drawn across Europe.

By the time 'Edward the peacemaker' died the following year a deeper Russian tragedy was already under way. The summer before the reunion party at Reval, Nicholas and Alexandra had taken a fat young woman named Anna Vyrubova on a fortnight's cruise in the Finnish fjords. A girl of no importance around the court, dowdy and tiresome, superstitious and servile, she attracted first Alexandra's attention, then her friendship, by

her very dependence. Alix was lonely and longing to be needed. They gossiped together and sang and played duets at the piano; before long Anna had become the Tsarina's most constant companion. They also had Faith in common, and particularly faith in the holy man, the *starets,* the country priest who was already an occasional visitor to the Imperial Palace – Rasputin.

From the mass of anecdote and conjecture which has accumulated around Rasputin, one surprising probability emerges: that he was basically an honest man. The Orthodox Church views sin differently from other Christian churches; in its canons there appears to be no absolute distinction between the good and the wicked, the blessed and the damned. There is no ritual of confession and absolution on earth; repentance is a more private matter, and every soul is acknowledged as a compound of righteousness and wrongfulness of which God will accept His share. One extreme sect, the Khlysty, believed that one should sin as much as possible so that one's repentance could be the greater and one's salvation the more resounding. Rasputin was influenced by the Khlysty, and nothing in his conduct really ran counter to the deepest Russian beliefs.

Nor is there the same categorical distinction between clergy and laity as in other Christian churches: a holy man is essentially a man who sees into the mysteries of God, who preaches and prays and may heal and prophesy and wander, like Rasputin, among his fellows. For all that he was a drunken rapist, coarse, boastful, treacherous and offensive, there is no reason to believe that Gregory Rasputin was a cynical charlatan, although most of his better-educated contemporaries thought so. Although he did not lack native shrewdness, the indications are that he believed profoundly that the universe is a holy mystery, that life is for living, and that God is not mocked – the beliefs of the Russian peasantry from which he came.

It is easy to understand what Alix saw in Rasputin. She had been morbidly religious as a girl, and since coming to Russia she had longed to be identified with the Russian spirit and to be the soul-mother of its simple people. By the tradition of the country, priests were admitted – earthy and smelling in their uncultivated holiness – into the homes of rich and poor and even into the Imperial palaces. No one thought it strange that Nicholas should

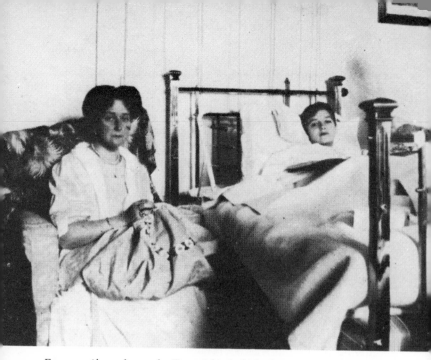

Empress Alexandra at the Tsarevich's bedside during a grave haemophilia crisis he suffered at Spala in the autumn of 1912

remark, 'I like to have a talk with Gregory, and invariably feel at peace with myself afterwards'.

To what extent Rasputin cultivated the Imperial family to do the will of God, or from natural ambition, it is harder to say; the two were probably entangled in his mind, and he enjoyed both the sacred and profane rewards. He also clearly believed in his own healing powers. He was undoubtedly a great hypnotist, and the hypnotic influence he exerted over the little Tsarevich Alexis may have done much or little to control the boy's bouts of bleeding, but certainly something. He also gave Alix comfort and guidance on which she came to depend utterly – as well as being her one available window on to the simple but mysterious world of the Great Russian people, of which she longed to be a part.

At some point it occurred to her that, if Rasputin could help her and her son, he might also help her husband. In their palaces at Tsarskoe Selo, or Peterhof or Livadia, or in the great Winter Palace at St Petersburg, the Tsar and his family lived behind a façade of grandiose court rooms in private apartments guarded by enormous, coloured and colourfully uniformed flunkeys. In their own suite Nicholas and Alix led a family existence completely segregated from the lives of their subjects. As she nibbled her plain English biscuits and he smoked his cigarettes and glanced at the books which he never had time to finish reading, the world outside went on in ways which they could not imagine. Rasputin came in from it, like a pilgrim, to advise them, and as the years went on he advised them more and more.

Stolypin, a practical and authoritarian man, had a very low opinion of Rasputin and did not approve of his interference. There were enough people working against him, particularly around the court, and Alexandra herself was critical and perhaps jealous of her husband's Chief Minister. It seemed to her a good idea to have Rasputin's opinion, and she arranged for the two men to take tea together. It was not a successful encounter. 'I began to feel an indescribable loathing for this vermin sitting opposite me,' Stolypin told Rodzianko, the President of the State Duma. The antipathy was mutual: Rasputin reported to the palace that Stolypin was not amenable to the will of God and from then on the Chief Minister's position began to weaken.

Nicholas was notorious for the inconstancy of his personal loyalties; as Wilhelm once said, 'The way to deal with him is to be the last to leave the room'. He began to feel that the more he saw of Stolypin the less he liked him. Without the Tsar's backing, Stolypin's role became impossible and he grew frustrated and ill. The end came for him in 1911. Early in the year he banished Rasputin from St Petersburg, and the Tsarina did not forgive him. As the Tsar became more distant, Stolypin's enemies closed in; he was not even given adequate police protection.

In September he accompanied Nicholas on a state visit to Kiev where, by some weird chance, Rasputin was in the crowd, shouting about the hand of death; and there Stolypin was shot dead in the Opera House, in full view of the Imperial box, by a young Jew who was probably an *okhrana* agent. No one of a calibre remotely approaching Stolypin's was ever the Tsar's Chief Minister again.

Chapter eleven

The Great Conflict

In June 1914 Franz Josef, alone at his desk at Bad Ischl, made a concession to his nephew and heir Franz Ferdinand: he allowed him to take his wife Sophie to Sarajevo, the capital of Bosnia.

Nearly everyone disliked Franz Ferdinand, a humourless, hectoring man of unappealing looks, who killed wild animals in large numbers; but he was conscientious and not unintelligent. As Franz Josef was eighty-four and the empire he had ruled for sixty-five years was in danger of dropping in pieces from his failing grasp, the unpalatable nephew would have to be either disposed of or accepted as ruler in the very near future. The army was already under his control and something like a shadow ministry was forming itself reluctantly around him; but Franz Josef continued to exclude him as far as possible from state affairs.

When not in his white baroque Belvedere palace in Vienna, Franz Ferdinand lived in the beautiful Villa d'Este near Venice and grew roses. To his credit he was deeply devoted to his own family, but his choice of wife was one of the many things not forgiven him, particularly by the Emperor. Sophie came from an aristocratic but poor Czech family and had been a lady at the court. In Franz Josef's mind she remained a lady-in-waiting; Franz Ferdinand was forced to marry her morganatically, their

Archduke Franz Ferdinand with his morganatic wife Sophie and their children, Ernst, Sophie and Max

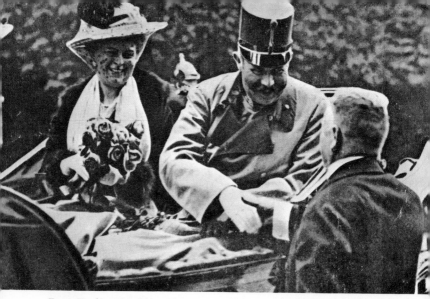

Franz Ferdinand and his wife in Sarajevo about an hour before their assassination on 28 June 1914

children were debarred from the Imperial succession, she was allowed no royal precedence, and insulted as much and as often as possible. It was thus an unusual honour for her to be allowed to accompany her husband on his state visit to Bosnia.

Franz Ferdinand had very clear ideas of how to manage the Empire. Principally he intended to turn the Dual Monarchy into a Triple Monarchy, in which the Slav inhabitants would be promoted to the same status as the Hungarians, a plan which commended itself to nobody. The Austrians themselves saw it as a further weakening of their hold as Imperial masters, the Hungarians as an encroachment on the privileged position which Andrassy had won for them, and the Slavs as a trick to bind them more closely to Vienna, when in fact they wanted complete independence in a Balkan union centred on Serbia and underwritten by their fellow-Slavs in Russia. But Franz Ferdinand was not one to tolerate opposition, and he was supported by Kaiser Wilhelm, who had recently visited him at Este, admired his wife and roses, and assured him that the way was open as Russia showed 'the spirit of a sick tom-cat'. Wilhelm, as usual, had little idea what he was starting.

Bosnia, now forcibly annexed by the Austrian Empire, was still dangerous territory, and Serbia, its neighbour to the east,

Archduke Karl

determined to keep it so; the secret Serbian terrorist organisation, the Black Hand, had agents trained and waiting in Sarajevo. It is possible, though not certain, that Franz Josef's officials in Vienna knew this and were not unwilling to send Franz Ferdinand and his wife, lightly guarded, to their likely deaths, and so provide an excuse for settling scores, once and for all, with the Slavs in the Balkans; but, whether planned or not, the result was the same.

On 28 June Franz Ferdinand and Sophie drove into Sarajevo and were shot dead in their car by a young assassin of the Serbian Black Hand, Gavrilo Princip. Franz Josef's first reaction was one of relief that the apostolic succession had been providentially readjusted: 'A Higher Power has restored that order which I myself was unable to maintain.' He much preferred his new heir, young Archduke Karl, and Franz Ferdinand and Sophie were buried quickly and with little honour.

Wilhelm was yachting at Kiel when he heard the news and hurried back to Potsdam; but, being assured that all was well, set off on a cruise of the Norwegian fjords. It was a fine summer. The Tsar and his family were on *their* yacht when they heard about the Sarajevo shooting, but were more concerned with family anxieties – the Tsarevich was ill again and Rasputin had been stabbed in the stomach by an infuriated woman and was unable to help. They continued their cruise.

The remarkable indifference of the three Emperors was a symptom of a much deeper ill which was to be their undoing. They were not only out of touch but in a sense no longer important. When in 1848, 1890 and 1894, Franz Josef, Wilhelm and Nicholas in turn opted for autocracy, they cut themselves off from their people and from those politicians who would have given them a constitutional role in national life, and relied increasingly on their armed forces to keep them in power. The 'dreadful militarism' which Vicky had feared had taken control of their destinies. Even Bismarck had warned the Austrian government, 'We must both take care that the privilege of giving political advice to our monarchs does not in fact slip out of our hands and pass over to the General Staffs'. By 1914 the military commanders were a dangerously powerful force within all three governments; policy was sacrificed to strategy, and the emperors themselves had become little more than figureheads.

In Vienna Field Marshal von Hötzendorff, although an able strategist, was recklessly hawkish in his demands: he was determined to make Franz Ferdinand's assassination an excuse for battering Serbia and the rest of the Balkan Slavs into submission while Russia was still too weak to risk a European war, and none of Franz Josef's civil ministers could stand against him. Von Hötzendorff relied on the threat that, under their old treaty, Germany would back Austria to keep Russia neutral, and on 4 July the Austrian government sent a request for such backing to Berlin, with a personal letter to Wilhelm from Franz Josef, who had by now been persuaded that the Sarajevo assassination was an affront to his Imperial dignity. 'The policy of peace which all European monarchs have pursued', he wrote, 'will be jeopardised as long as this gang of criminal agitators in Belgrade* goes unpunished.'

---

* The capital of Serbia, and so the centre of Slav resistance in the Balkans.

In Berlin the Chief of General Staff von Moltke (nephew of the older and greater Moltke) and his fellow generals felt that the sooner Austria dealt with Serbia the better, since Russia was unready to fight yet; so Wilhelm assured the Austrians of German support, but begged them to keep the conflict local. In spite of his grandiose dreams of a world-wide empire, Wilhelm was often frightened, and in his more perceptive moments he saw more clearly than his fellow-emperors the way things were going.

In 1912 Wilhelm had written:

Russia seems anxious to support Serb aspirations and could in consequence get into a situation with Austria which made war inevitable. That would bring about the *Casus foederis* for Germany – since Vienna would be attacked by Petersburg – according to the Treaty. This entails mobilisation and war on two fronts for Germany, i.e. in order to march against Moscow, Paris must first be taken. Paris would undoubtedly be supported by London. That would mean Germany having to fight for her existence against three Great Powers with everything at stake and possibly in the end succumb.

He was horribly right, but by 1914 he was the victim of his own earlier policies and the prisoner of military necessity, and in any case his moments of perception were soon clouded.

One striking phrase of Wilhelm's 1912 statement was that 'in order to march against Moscow, Paris must first be taken'. This was not the logic of statesmanship but of the German High Command. Since Bismarck's time, Germany had feared a simultaneous attack from east and west, and after the Triple Entente of 1908 Germans had felt themselves malevolently encircled by France and Russia on land and by Britain at sea: it was as though Wilhelm's paranoia had spread to his people. Against this, they were aware that their own military and naval powers were approaching a level which could make them military masters of Europe, and perhaps later of the world, if they struck in the right place at the right time. Their military plan had been drawn up a generation before by an earlier Chief of General Staff, von Schlieffen, and they had made curiously little effort to modify it. Under the Schlieffen Plan, the main German army would sweep through Belgium and northern France on to Paris, and knock out France before turning east to deal with Russia.

This ignored the possibility of keeping France out of any war in eastern Europe, and also the certainty that Britain would join the forces against them if Belgium were invaded. It assumed too that Austria-Hungary would be at war with Russia from the start and would hold the eastern front steady until the main German army was ready to attack the Russians.

With so inflexible an arrangement the first move would make the whole operation inevitable, regardless of diplomacy, humanity or common sense. The German government left it to Vienna to make the first move and the Austrians felt sufficiently emboldened to draft an unacceptable ultimatum to the Serbs, as a preliminary to invading Serbia. The Austrian government delayed sending the ultimatum for several days, partly because of Franz Josef's reluctance to move hastily, but mainly for the purely strategic purpose of catching Russia on the wrong foot.

The Russian military leaders were less bent on instant war – they would rather have waited until 1917 – but their automatic reaction to the menace growing in the west was to fight, and they gradually imposed their view on Nicholas and his hesitant civilian ministers. A British naval squadron had just called at Kronstadt, and the French President, Poincaré, was visiting St Petersburg in the battleship *France*: after years of isolation, Russia appeared to have strong and willing allies, and the Russian military lobby was determined not to back down in the Balkans.

Nicholas, returning from holiday to greet the French President, had no idea that anything unusual was afoot, and the Austrians did not deliver their ultimatum to Serbia until after Poincaré left St Petersburg, in order to prevent any top-level discussion of it between the Russians and their principal ally. It came on the morning of 24 July when the battleship *France* was steaming away down the Gulf of Finland. Sazonov, the Russian Foreign Minister, reading it, said simply, 'It is the European war', but Nicholas did not believe it. He promised the Serbian government to support them if necessary, but advised them to accept the ultimatum, and sent a telegram to Wilhelm begging him to restrain the Austrians.

Wilhelm was back from his cruise and terribly worried, but the German High Command had no intention of restraining the Austrians, and when the Serbian acceptance of almost the entire contents of the Austrian government's ultimatum reached

Vienna, Franz Josef's ministers rejected it and declared war. On 29 July von Hötzendorff's artillery began shelling Belgrade. For the rest of the month Wilhelm and Nicholas exchanged agonised telegrams, each imploring the other to help contain the fighting in the Balkans, but their minds were divided and in any case the power had gone out of their hands: the demands of their military advisers' timetable bore inexorably down on them.

Alexandra also received a telegram – from Rasputin, who was recuperating in Siberia: 'Let Papa not plan war, for with the war will come the end of Russia and yourselves and you will lose to the last man.' Nicholas ignored it. Under pressure from his generals, he ordered a partial mobilisation of the Russian forces – to cover the Austrian front only – but Russia's mobilisation arrangements were so widespread and cumbersome that what Nicholas intended would have made a later, rapid full mobilisation impossible. The generals therefore opted for the full plan, without telling him.

When Wilhelm received the news he wrote on the dispatch, 'Then I must mobilise too!' and also made inquiries in London to establish Britain's attitude. The British government prevaricated, still hoping to steer clear of the continental whirlpool, and then warned Germany, too late, that Britain would be against her. This was too much for Wilhelm. 'Now we get what the English consider to be gratitude,' he wrote, and threw in his lot with his soldiers.

He still hoped, however, that Russia would draw back, although his government had already sent its declaration of war to St Petersburg. Just before midnight on 31 July the German ambassador visited Sazonov with a demand that Russian mobilisation be stopped within twelve hours. He could not believe that Russia would not withdraw, although Sazonov had taken him by the shoulders and told him, 'Russia means it!' When the answer was an unequivocal No, he handed Sazonov the German declaration of war and left in tears. In the early hours of the next morning a delayed telegram from Wilhelm reached Nicholas, begging him to hold back his troops. Its intention, Nicholas decided, 'was to shake my resolution, disconcert me and inspire me to some absurd and dishonourable step. . . . I felt that all was over for ever between me and William.'

On 1 August a state of war existed between Russia and Germany, and the Schlieffen Plan was put into action. On the second an ultimatum to Belgium was followed by a German invasion, on the third Germany declared war on France and on the fourth Britain on Germany. The long, armed truce between the European empires was over. The solid worth of the German people, the charm of Austria and the warm humanity of Russia were all burnt away in a blaze of hatred fanned by their national presses. On 6 August Franz Josef sat at his desk at Bad Ischl and signed a declaration of war against Russia; but it no longer mattered greatly what he did.

Germany's war plan depended on quick victories, and the High Command had no doubt of winning them. 'Lunch in Paris, dinner in St Petersburg,' Wilhelm announced hopefully. In the first days of August a million and a half German soldiers advanced through Belgium and pushed the French army back towards Paris more swiftly even than in 1870. The entire British army, of only six divisions, was swept back with the French. Wilhelm dashed about in his Imperial train and complained that 'the General Staff tells me nothing and never asks my advice. I drink tea, go for walks and saw wood, which pleases my suite. The only one who is a bit kind to me is the Chief of the Railway Department.' They did well enough without him, and by the end of August the German army was ranged along the River Marne, just north of Paris.

Nicholas's immediate contributions were to rename St Petersburg Petrograd, and to forbid the sale of alcohol. More important, he wanted to direct the Russian Army as Commander-in-Chief. At the outbreak of war there was an enormous and unexpected rallying of popular support to the Tsar's cause. Although neither the military command nor the Russian people saw any prospect of easy victory, or even of victory at all, they embraced the war with a kind of awed fatalism, and Nicholas was cheered by an immense crowd outside the Winter Palace.

He was dissuaded, however, by all his ministers from taking command of the army, and appointed a cousin, the Grand Duke Nicholas Nicholayevich, as Commander-in-Chief. The Grand Duke was a soldier of considerable reputation, who had been the sponsor of a new cadre of enlightened and modern-minded officers produced by the Imperial staff college since the Japanese war. He was a towering and impressive figure. The French

Grand Duke Nicholas

Nicholas II with Grand Duke Nicholas on the day war was declared, 1 August 1914

ambassador to Petrograd reported, 'His whole being exuded a fierce energy,' and even his most uncompromising German opponent, General von Ludendorff, admitted, 'The Grand Duke was really a great soldier and strategist, but what perhaps counted for even more than that, was that he was a man of splendid moral courage.'

He was also a constitutional royalist and the Duma itself approved of him. On 8 August the Duma endorsed the government's policy and dissolved itself to concentrate on national Red Cross work organised by the *zemstva;* even the few socialist deputies, led by Kerensky, supported the war and only abstained from voting on the military budget. Grand Duke Nicholas, embracing the Duma's President in a fervour of patriotic gratitude, declared, 'Now, Rodzianko, I am your friend till death. I will do anything for the Duma.'

But with the Duma gone civil government remained entirely in the old, incapable hands of Nicholas's appointed ministers, of whom the most disastrous happened to be Sukhomlinov, the Minister for War. 'Sukhomlinov, who was later to be actually tried for treason . . . without question was extraordinarily light-headed, superficial and casual.'[1] He was also jealous of the Grand Duke and more than any other one man was responsible for the appalling unpreparedness of the Russian army. 'Russia was hopelessly short of heavy artillery. . . . As to ammunition, there was in peace time practically no reserve. . . . There were hardly any aeroplanes at all, and a great shortage of telephones, telegraph and wireless. Transport was so bad that the *zemstvo* Red Cross had to supplement it by national effort.'[2] Nor was the Grand Duke well served by his subordinate commanders. Against that, he had an army of nearly a million and a half men of legendary bravery and endurance and a reserve force of over three million.

By the middle of August the French were demanding an immediate Russian offensive to relieve the pressure on their own army. Both the Tsar and the Grand Duke felt compelled to honour their alliance, and on 17 August the first and second Russian armies, on the north of the line, advanced into east Prussia. At the same time an Austro-Hungarian army a million strong attacked Serbia and Russia in the south, but were held and forced back.

Prussian alarm was great: the prospect of Cossack hordes descending on Berlin while the main German army's back was turned moved von Moltke to remove two army corps from the Western Front and send them east. One of Germany's greatest soldiers, Field Marshal von Hindenburg – veteran of Sadowa and Sedan – was recalled from retirement and appointed Commander-in-Chief of the Eastern Front, with Ludendorff as his Chief-of-Staff. Under their command, the reinforced German Eastern Army counter-attacked. In September, out-generalled and out-gunned, the Russian Second Army was destroyed at Tannenburg and the First Army in the battle of the Masurian Lakes, with a loss of nearly 200,000 men.

All the same, the Russian line re-formed, and held. In France the weakened German army lost the battle of the Marne and was forced back to a line which remained more or less static for almost four years. Moltke's quick victory had not materialised, in east or west, and Europe settled down to a war of slow and terrible attrition.

Chapter twelve

'Tell the King the Sky is Falling'

While the Germans and the Western Allies faced each other from the Belgian coast to the Swiss mountains, in the bloody slogging-match of the Western Front, yet bloodier fighting continued between the German, Austrian and Russian empires. 'The struggle upon the Eastern Front is incomparably the greatest war in history,' Churchill wrote. 'In its scale, in its slaughter, in the exertions of the combatants, in its military kaleidoscope, it far surpasses in magnitude and intensity all similar human episodes. It is also the most mournful conflict of which there is record. All three empires, both sides, victim and vanquished, were ruined.'[1]

In the early spring of 1915 the Russians attacked in the south, fighting their way over the Carpathian mountains into the Danube valley in an attempt to knock Austria out of the war. The Germans, meanwhile, had decided to finish off Russia that summer, and in April Hindenburg and Ludendorff, with reinforcements withdrawn from the stalemate on the Western Front, launched a major offensive against the centre of the Russian line. Within four hours 700,000 shells fell on the Russian front line. 'The elementary Russian trenches were practically wiped out and so, to all intents and purposes, was human life in that area.'[2] Russian Headquarters reported: 'The army is drowning in its own blood.'

A Field Mass in Russian Poland during the war

Russian Cossacks on the march in 1914

For the rest of the spring and summer, the Russian troops fell back eastwards, giving up all their earlier gains. Recruits were drafted into the line unarmed, to take rifles from the fallen; and many engagements were fought without shells or food. Grand Duke Nicholas called the supply and training services 'beneath contempt', but himself added to the chaos by evacuating entire populations who wandered, homeless and hopeless, behind the lines. In Petrograd, in June, Sukhomlinov was replaced by a new War Minister, Polivanov, who enormously increased supplies; but there were never enough.

The Grand Duke now had two good generals of his own supervising the front, Brusilov in the south and Alexeyev in the north, and under them the Russians retreated slowly, skilfully and bravely, often without artillery or even cartridges, counter-attacking with only swords and bayonets. 'Sometimes,' Hindenburg wrote, 'we had to remove the mounds of enemy corpses from before our trenches in order to get a clear field of fire against fresh assaulting waves.'

In the first full year of war Nicholas lost four million of his subjects in battle. Yet the Germans failed. All their effort, Ludendorff confessed, 'again resulted only in a tactical success'. By the end of that summer's fighting what was left of the Russian army had formed a new front, from Riga on the Baltic in the north to the neutral Rumanian frontier in the south – another six hundred contested miles of mud and horror.

The Grand Duke's time was nearly run: he had incurred the hostility of the Empress. A change had come over Alexandra at the outbreak of the war. 1914 found her, at forty-two, an invalidish lady, suffering from an unspecified heart condition, and a prey to neuralgia and nervous headaches. 'It is too sad and painful,' wrote the Dowager Empress in some exasperation, 'to see Alix always ailing and incapable of taking part in anything.' But at the outbreak of hostilities Alix threw herself into hospital work with all the fervour of her highly-strung temperament. Like her mother and her Aunt Vicky, who had reorganised hospitals and nursing services in their adopted countries, she had a strong practical streak. Not content with organising, she took a course in nursing and, in her Red Cross uniform, daily bandaged gangrenous wounds, and assisted at operations with almost morbid interest. 'Our first big amputation today. Whole arm cut off,' she wrote to Nicholas, away on one of his visits to Stavka (the Russian Army headquarters). She told a friend she had never felt so well.

Empress Alexandra with her daughters, Olga, Tatiana, Marie and Anastasia, about 1910

Nicholas II at Stavka

For the first year of the war the Empress took little interest in its conduct; she had always regarded the affairs of government as an intrusion on the family life of her devoted 'hubby'. But from the outset she showed a dislike of the Grand Duke, and her verbal campaign against him increased in intensity as the months went on. The Commander-in-Chief was a popular figure, a marked physical contrast to the short, slight person of the Emperor. Alix wanted to see her husband Commander-in-Chief. Moreover, the Grand Duke had spoken against Rasputin, and that was an unforgivable crime. 'I have absolutely no faith in N,' she wrote; '. . . having gone against a Man of God, his work can't be blessed or his advice good.' Later, 'Nobody knows who is Emperor now. . . . It is as though N settles all.'

Nicholas respected his Commander-in-Chief, but Alexandra's 'smear campaign' gradually eroded his trust. Also, he wanted more than ever to assume the supreme command himself. With the war going badly, his instinct was to be at Stavka. At the end of August 1915, three weeks after the fall of Warsaw, the Emperor and Empress visited a cathedral in Petrograd and knelt in prayer for some hours before a certain miraculous icon of the Virgin. That evening, a Council of Ministers was called at the Alexander Palace, at which Nicholas presided, clutching an icon pressed into his hand by the ubiquitous Anna Vyrubova. He informed the Council that he intended to take over forthwith as Commander-in-Chief of the Armies with General Alexeyev as Chief-of-Staff. In vain the appalled ministers pointed out that he could not govern the country at 500 miles distance from the capital, that he would personally become associated with military reverses. He stuck to his decision. A tactful letter was sent to the Grand Duke, and two days later the Emperor left for Stavka.

'It is the beginning of the great glory of your reign,' wrote Alexandra ecstatically. 'Sleep well, my Sunshine, Russia's Saviour.'

In Petrograd an extremely disturbed Council was left to govern the country. Eight of them had collectively asked to resign in protest against the Tsar's decision, but their resignations were not accepted. The real power of the government was vested in its autocratic ruler; in this medievally governed country, with the Tsar away, his place could only be taken by his totally inexperienced wife. Nicholas could not foresee the immense and fatal power she would eventually wield.

At first, writing from Stavka, he asked her to help him by 'speaking to the ministers and watching them'. Alexandra felt diffident about her new role; but not for long. She had never overcome her shyness and awkwardness in personal relations, but her arrogance was deeply rooted. She had seen her husband

Rasputin surrounded by his 'court'

Rasputin

anointed Emperor and Autocrat of All the Russias, and she *knew* unshakeably that he was divinely appointed, and answerable only to God. And God's Russian representative was at her elbow, ready to advise her. During the winter of 1915 Anna Vyrubova was badly hurt in a train accident, and was apparently brought back to life by Rasputin's hypnotic powers – an act which entrenched him more firmly in the Empress's favour.

Alix had perhaps the worst temperament for the mother of an afflicted child. She suffered anguish when he suffered, and when he was well her perpetual anxiety was frustrating to the lively and otherwise very normal little boy. Rasputin's presence gave her some peace of mind. She had absolute faith in his powers of healing her son, and, with Nicholas away, she began to rely on his 'God-sent' perspicacity in choosing ministers and making political decisions. The *starets* was a huge, black-bearded, often dirty man, with light, brilliant eyes whose magnetism shines out even from photographs. It is hard to believe that his attraction for Alexandra was as purely spiritual as she thought it to be. His influence at Court was widely used. People from all walks of life queued on his staircase in the hope of getting a scrap of paper with a few ill-written lines and his signature – the passport to places at court, promotions or contracts.

Rasputin's way of putting forward new ministers was scarcely more selective. The essential requirement for a candidate was that he should be, as Alexandra put it, 'one of us'. And she was ruthless in persuading the Tsar to remove from office anyone who had criticised Rasputin, or tried to expose the corruption and profiteering going on among his protégés. Soon she could hardly wait for his replies, and demanded that he should telegraph his agreement.

The ministers who had asked to resign and criticised the Tsar's decision to become Commander-in-Chief soon found themselves out of office. The new ones could not work with the Chief Minister, old Goremykin, so Alexandra was faced with the task of recommending a new premier. The first candidate failed the test of taking tea with Rasputin. The next was put forward by a protégé of the *starets* and was immediately popular with the Empress. Boris Stürmer was an elderly bureaucrat, of German origin. His contemporaries had nothing good to say of him. 'A nonentity', 'worse than a mediocrity', 'false and double-faced' were some opinions in political circles. But the trusting Nicholas found that he had 'unlimited confidence in Stürmer', and the new appointment was made – a disastrous one for Russia. 'All serious critics agree in dating the beginning of the ruin from the miserable end of the constitutional crisis in September 1915, and the pace was vastly accelerated on the advent of Stürmer. . . . Equally, it is from the autumn of 1915 that we must date the serious growth of national discontent. . . .'[3]

During the next sixteen months the rapid changes in ministries became almost ludicrous. Men of ability and integrity were replaced by nominees of Rasputin, who usually had little to recommend them except their respect, real or simulated, for the Man of God. One of the first to go was Polivanov, the able Minister of War. Since he had replaced Sukhomlinov, the training and equipment of the army had vastly improved, but Alexandra suspected he was 'our Friend's enemy', and when he voiced strong objections to Rasputin's allowance of four high-powered War Office cars, she sent a barrage of letters to Stavka. 'Get rid of Polivanov. . . . Lovey, don't dawdle, make up your mind.' She soon got her way.

The Foreign Minister, Sazonov, was on holiday in Finland, believing himself to have brought off a diplomatic coup with the Tsar's complete approval, when news of *his* dismissal reached him: Nicholas had an ambiguous way of parting company with those in his service. The post of Foreign Minister was now taken over by Stürmer in addition to the premiership. The news caused especial consternation to the Allies' ambassadors, who would have to work with a man whom they despised.

Not content with choosing ministers, the Empress and her Friend began taking an interest in running the war. Alexandra asked her husband about military plans – 'our Friend is so anxious to know' – and soon she was passing on Rasputin's advice, based on ideas that came to him in dreams. Nor was Rasputin above talking openly about it to others when drunk. Nicholas sometimes made mild attempts to stop this traffic in military secrets – 'I beg you not to tell anyone about it – not even our Friend' – but he still gave the required information, and sometimes passed on the *starets'* suggestions to Alexeyev, who seemed unimpressed.

There is no evidence that Rasputin was, as was widely believed, in the pay of the Germans. He had a deep fear of the war, as he had of reform, because he recognised in it a threat to

Nicholas II with his son Alexis

the existing order of the kingdom of the Holy Tsar. However much he enjoyed manipulating people, however little he may have thought of Nicholas, his orthodoxy demanded a holy bond between Tsar and people, and his peasant's instincts told him when that was in danger. They also opposed him to the mass sacrifice of lives. He loved Russian-ness more than he loved money – he had always enough for his needs – and it is unlikely that he was a deliberate traitor. His objections to the generals' conduct of the war were always on grounds of humanity. 'Our Friend', Alix wrote, 'finds better one should not advance too obstinately as the losses will be too great.' And it was Rasputin who reported, 'The villages are looking empty'. But, whatever his motives, his influence was politically calamitous.

The Tsar was an increasingly lonely figure. At first he had seemed happy at Stavka, where there were 'no ministers, no troublesome questions demanding thought'. He had his son with him, whose lively eleven-year-old presence lightened his daily life. But the troublesome questions followed him, Alexis went home after a serious nose-bleed, and he was losing the friendly respect of those around him. As he became more and more enslaved by the ideas of his wife and Rasputin, honest men lost their trust in him. Gradually he withdrew into himself. While soldiers were being slaughtered in their hundreds of thousands, their Tsar was writing long, nostalgic letters to his wife, noting changes in the weather and being moved to tears by a sentimental novel, *Boy Blue,* which was a great favourite with the Imperial couple.

Their remarkable twenty-year love affair continued. From her Mauve Boudoir, where she interviewed ministers among drapery and knick-knacks, Alix dashed off her letters, telling him that she 'kissed his cushion' and 'yearned for his embrace'. She sent him '1000 burning kisses' and was his own, his very own Wifie. Nicholas wrote less ardently, but with patient sympathy for her many ills, both physical and emotional. The plight of his country might be beyond his imaginative grasp, but he could enter into 'Sunny's' morbid distress over a dying officer.

Thanks to the work of the deposed Polivanov, the army was in good shape and good heart again by the summer of 1916; but in the rear there was now widespread discontent. Food prices soared, food queues lengthened, and fuel also was scarce; people were cold and hungry and saw no prospect of an end to the war.

And yet the country was not basically short of food. An inefficient government, quite unable to deal with the problems of transport and supply, was the root cause of the trouble. On a June evening that year, Rodzianko, President of the Duma – another of Russia's great bear-like men – took occasion at a party given by Stürmer to trounce the government in stentorian tones. He told them they were incapable of leadership, and that their disputes and intrigues paralysed the work of administration. In your senseless search for a bogey revolution,' he concluded, 'you are murdering the living soul of the people and creating unrest . . . which sooner or later may breed an actual revolution.'

In the autumn it became necessary to create a new Minister of the Interior. For this vital post, controlling the food supply and also the police forces, Rasputin and the Empress suggested a small, sleek, affable man named Protopopov, yet another native of Simbirsk. Nicholas hesitated over the appointment, remarking mildly, 'Our Friend's opinions of people are sometimes very strange,' but he soon agreed. Most people regarded it as another disastrous choice. The Duma met and gave voice to an unprecedented storm of criticism of the government. Stürmer was their chief target, but Rasputin was openly attacked and, by implication, the Empress. The great surge of unrest in Russia was beginning to break through the surface.

Many people tried to warn the Tsar of the seriousness of the situation. At Stavka Alexeyev repeatedly urged him to get rid of Stürmer; so did other staff officers close to him. Members of the Imperial family who were beginning to see the writing on the wall begged him to give Russia a strong government and to be its constitutional head. The Tsar listened politely, smoking a cigarette – and did nothing. With obstinate loyalty he clung to the narrow course laid down for him by his ancestors, and underlined by his wife in every letter – to keep the autocratic rights of a Tsar and hand them on unweakened to his son. At the beginning of November the British ambassador visited him to add to his serious warning of disaster, mentioning Stürmer and Protopopov specifically. Nicholas at last gave in, to the limited extent of dismissing Stürmer.

The new premier, Trepov, promoted from being Transport Minister, was not brilliant, but he had some integrity, and he was determined to purge the government of Rasputin's nominees. Protopopov's removal seemed the most urgent. He was still in high favour with Alexandra. 'He venerates our Friend,' she wrote enthusiastically. But Protopopov could not even carry out the instructions, often shrewdly sensible ones in relation to food supplies, which Rasputin sent to him through the Empress; yet he had delusions of grandeur, and thought he would 'save Russia' by provoking, then crushing, a revolution.

Trepov went to Stavka, had an amicable interview with the Tsar, and came away with the impression that his suggested ministerial changes were to be implemented. Nicholas explained his decision to Alexandra, adding, 'I beg, do not drag Our Friend into this. The responsibility is with me.' It was a vain hope. Alexandra immediately sent off a flood of pleas and exhortations, pulling out every emotional stop: 'I entreat you, don't go and change Protopopov now. . . . I may not be clever enough but I have a strong feeling. . . . I am but a woman fighting for her Master and her Child. . . . Quieten me, promise, forgive. I am fighting for your reign and Baby's future.' In her eyes, Trepov was trying to isolate the Tsar and herself from their friends and must be fought. 'It is war with them,' she insisted. She was afraid Nicholas would give in. 'I wish I could pour my will into your veins!' was one of her Lady Macbeth-like utterances.

Nicholas promised to delay his decision until she arrived at Stavka on a prearranged visit. Two days later she was there. They talked, and for once argued passionately in the privacy of Nicholas's room. By the time the Empress left, she had won her case. Protopopov stayed in office. Trepov was curtly ordered to work with the ministers assigned to him. Desperate, he tried to bribe Rasputin, which only amused the *starets* and deepened Alexandra's distrust of Trepov. His days as premier were numbered.

Alexandra wrote jubilantly to Nicholas of 'beautiful times coming for you and for Russia', but to others it seemed as though the last hope of uniting Russia under a responsible government had gone. Alexandra's sister Ella, widow of the Grand Duke Serge, was persuaded to leave the convent she had founded after her husband's death to urge Alexandra to dismiss Rasputin. The visit was a failure. At the mention of Rasputin, Alix abruptly brought their meeting to an end. They parted coldly, Ella reputedly murmuring 'Poor Nicky, poor Russia' as she left. The Empress was locked in an impenetrable dream. She wrote to her husband, urging him to 'be Peter the Great, Ivan the Terrible' and to 'crush them all under you'.

Throughout the country Alexandra was hated only less than Rasputin. Plots to kidnap or kill the pair of them were openly discussed in Petrograd. In December the Duma was in session again, and in a vehement speech one of the Deputies, Purishkevich, spoke of 'dark forces' behind the recent appointments, and called on members to throw themselves at the Tsar's feet and beg leave to open his eyes to reality. Listening intently from the visitors' box was Felix Yussoupov, a young relative of the Tsar whose plans for Rasputin's assassination were more serious than most. The next morning, he went to call on Purishkevich.

On 30 December there were rumours of a drunken party at Yussoupov's house, of shots in the night and bloodstains on the snow. Alexandra wrote a disjointed, agitated letter to her husband. 'We are sitting together – you can imagine our feelings – thoughts – our Friend has disappeared. . . . I cannot and won't believe He has been killed. God have mercy . . .'

The Tsar was at a staff meeting when he received the letter. He telegraphed his shock and horror, but did not seem unduly depressed; nor did he, as Alexandra requested, leave for Tsarskoe Selo. Two days later, Rasputin's body was found under the ice in the Neva. His murder had been a protracted, amateurish business; finally, he had died of drowning. A letter secretly written by him in the last days of the year – and of his life – foresaw his own death and much else. Written apparently to the Tsar, it said, 'I feel I shall leave life before 1 January. . . . If I am killed by common assassins . . . you, Tsar of Russia, have nothing to fear. . . . But if I am murdered by nobles, and if they shed my blood . . . then no one of your family, that is to say, none of your children or relations will remain alive for more than two years. They will be killed by the Russian people.'

When the news of his death spread, strangers embraced each other in the streets with wild joy, and the murderers – Yussoupov, Purishkevich, and the Grand Duke Dmitry (another member of the Imperial family) – were hailed as heroes. In the euphoria of that crisp January morning there were many who felt Russia had been saved.

But it soon became apparent that nothing was changed. The Tsar came back to Tsarskoe Selo for a prolonged leave; the royal murderers were banished; Protopopov continued to be the only minister in the Empress's confidence; and the country continued to be governed from her Mauve Boudoir. Incredibly, the main telephone of the palace was there; and even when the Tsar received visiting dignitaries alone in his study, they had an uncomfortable feeling that the Empress was listening behind a curtained alcove.

After her first shock Alexandra had achieved a surprising composure; she was perhaps sustained by the thought that her 'dear martyr' was praying for her on high. The ever-ingratiating Protopopov claimed to be in touch with him. But events were at last having their effect on Nicholas. Those who had interviews with him in these winter months noticed his haggard face, his helpless, at times vacant, expression.

Still there were desperate attempts to get through to this doomed, sleep-walking couple. The Grand Duke Alexander Mikhailovich, a gay companion of Nicholas's youth and now father-in-law of Felix Yussoupov, left his home in Kiev to tell them both they had no right to drag their relatives 'down a precipice', and to beg Nicholas to set up a constitutional government. The French and English ambassadors each called on the Tsar to urge the same thing. As always, Nicholas listened with courtesy, but they could not penetrate his shell of fatalism and lethargy. The French ambassador had the impression that the Tsar had 'abdicated inwardly and is now resigned to disaster'.

On 7 January Rodzianko, at his own urgent request, had an audience with the Tsar. The President of the Duma was a faintly absurd figure in his fussy self-importance but, although Alexandra thought him a dangerous radical who should be sent to Siberia, he was a loyal monarchist. He told Nicholas of the dangerous mood of unrest among the people and of the great desire, now uniting all political parties, for a responsible government, free of the Empress's hated influence. He urged the Tsar not to compel people to choose between him and a responsible government. In Rodzianko's own words:

> The Emperor pressed his head between his hands, then said: 'Is it possible that for twenty-two years I have tried to act for the best, and for twenty-two years it was all a mistake?'
>
> It was a hard moment. With a great effort at self-control, I replied: 'Yes, your Majesty, for twenty-two years you followed a wrong course.'[4]

Did Nicholas have a moment of truth? If he did, it was too late. He bid Rodzianko a courteous farewell, and they went their several ways, the President to his clamouring Duma, Nicholas to the Mauve Boudoir.

The Tsar was not alone in trouble. Before the end of 1916 the last bitter waves in a lifetime of misfortune had overwhelmed Franz Josef: 'the abstract monarch', as Herman Broch called him, 'capable of taking upon himself the awe-inspiring dignity of absolute loneliness'.

Italy was now in the war against Austria, draining men and supplies from the Eastern Front. A Russian spring offensive under General Brusilov had penetrated deep into the Empire, and Austria-Hungary was only saved by German troops. From then on Austria was no longer an independent power and was listed in Berlin as a German prize of war. The Emperor's army, decimated and despised, had taken most of Austria-Hungary's able-bodied men, and the blood-loss continued; his cities faced winter shortages of food and fuel; his subject peoples grew restive again from despair; and Austrians themselves were looking for a way to end both the war and the régime.

In October the Austrian Prime Minister was assassinated in a Vienna café, and a month later death took Franz Josef himself. He died from bronchitis in his Schönbrunn palace, complaining, 'I am behind with my work'. Karl, an amiable and sensible young man, took his place; but the Dual Monarchy was already in ruins. 'I took over the throne under the most difficult conditions and I am leaving it under even worse ones,' Franz Josef said on his deathbed.

Warfare, not revolt, was crippling all the great Empires. Their arbitrary and imposed governments, based on antique administrative methods, were devoured by the very military machines they had created. Not only in Russia and Austria, but in every European state, the enormous strains of mechanised modern war were proving too great for the powers which had begun it. In France in 1916 there was mutiny in the army; in Britain the Liberal administration which had entered the war was overthrown by Lloyd George and a more radical government; only the German government remained unscathed because, of all the old Imperial systems, Germany's was the most efficient.

But even there the pressures were mounting, and in July 1916 Wilhelm dismissed his army command and promoted Hinden-

Franz Josef

The German High Command. Paul von Hindenburg and Erik von Ludendorff

burg to Chief of General Staff, with Ludendorff as his Quarter-master General. 'Henceforward he was forced by two deter-mined men – or rather by one man too stolid to lose his nerve and by another in whom the lust for having his own way came to acquire pathological dimensions. The Supreme War Lord from now on had less say than ever in the military field.'[5] Hindenburg and Ludendorff had one common aim – to prosecute and win the war at all costs and by any means. 'Gradually the baneful pair swept internal opposition aside.'[6] By the beginning of 1917, in spite of Wilhelm's objections and hesitations, the German government had taken two grisly decisions – to open unre-stricted U-boat warfare, and to tip Russia over the brink into revolution. Wilhelm had, in fact, been putting out peace feelers secretly to Nicholas, but Nicholas had rejected them; the Kaiser now had to accept the agonising alternative of seeing his fellow-sovereign humbled, in order to put Russia out of the war.

Since 1914 Wilhelm's government had been playing with the idea of weakening its enemies by fomenting revolt behind their lines – in British India, in the Ukraine, and in Russia itself – and for this purpose had put several million marks into the hands of various adventurers, one of whom was Trotsky's former colleague, Parvus. Parvus now called himself Helfhand and was encouraged by Berlin to set up an organisation to plan a revolution in Russia. In May 1915 Parvus went to see Lenin, who was now a disappointed and impoverished middle-aged exile in Switzerland. Of all the socialist leaders, Lenin was the only one to oppose the war outright. It seemed to him that the 'imperialist war' should be turned to civil war and that out of the chaos revolution would emerge. He still had a few Bolshevik adherents in Russia but was out of touch with them and felt isolated and aimless. He did once have a chance of speaking at a socialist convention and set off on his bicycle, thinking about it, but rode into the back of a tram and was taken home with concussion.

'We sat in the libraries more diligently than ever, we took walks as usual, but all this could not remove the feeling of being cooped up in this democratic cage. Somewhere beyond, a revolutionary struggle was mounting, life was astir, but it was all so far away,' Krupskaya wrote. 'Ilyich searched everywhere for some way of earning money.'[7] Although she was often ill, Krupskaya took a job in a refugee bureau to pay the rent. Yet Lenin distrusted Parvus and would have nothing to do with him.

In March 1915 another German-paid revolutionary, with better credentials, arrived in Switzerland from Berlin. He was Alexander Keskuela, an Estonian socialist, and that September he handed the Germans Lenin's proposals for making peace 'in the event of the Bolsheviks obtaining power in Russia,'[8] and Lenin received some money. Lenin's conditions hinged on the creation of a Russian republic, but his motives were not patriotic. 'It's not a matter of Russia,' he once said, 'I spit on her. That is merely a stage through which we are passing on the way to World Revolution.' He still had little hope. In January 1917 he told a meeting in Zürich, 'We of the older generation may not live to see the decisive battles of this coming revolution'.

The revolution which broke out in Russia a few weeks later took the German government and Lenin equally by surprise. A revolutionary friend brought him the news, 'after dinner, when Ilyich was getting ready to leave for the library, and I had finished the dishes', as Krupskaya remembered, and they all went down to the lake where 'on the shore all the newspapers were hung up as soon as they came out'.[9] As soon as he was convinced, Lenin made feverish efforts to reach Russia; but it was only after nearly a month of agonised negotiation that the German government provided a special train to take a mixed party of Russian revolutionaries across Germany and then through Sweden and Finland to Petrograd. Of the nineteen Bolsheviks among them, one was Lenin. 'In the middle of April 1917 the Germans took a sombre decision,' Churchill wrote portentously. 'They transported Lenin in a sealed truck like a plague bacillus from Switzerland into Russia.'[10]

Chapter thirteen
Revolution

The Tsar was at Stavka when the Russian revolution began in Petrograd early in March 1917. Held fast in the hard grey-and-white cold of winter, remote from the sources of food and fuel, full of political unrest, and garrisoned by dissatisfied troops, the Russian capital lay like a primed bomb in the snow. In the Duma Kerensky proclaimed: 'The ministers are but fleeting shadows. . . . To prevent a catastrophe the Tsar himself must be removed, by terrorist methods if there is no other way.'

On 10 March Protopopov, totally unable to cope with the violence in the streets, telephoned to Stavka. Nicholas replied, 'I command that the disorders in the capital shall be stopped tomorrow, as they are inadmissible at the heavy time of war with Germany and Austria,' and ordered troops to Petrograd. But the troops were no longer on his side; within two days the garrison was fraternising with the workers. By 12 March rebellious crowds had taken control of the city.

In many ways 1917 was a replay of 1905, with the same main characters in the same positions: Nicholas still stood for autocracy, Milyukov for a liberal constitutional monarchy, Kerensky – now a major political figure – for the moderate Socialist Revolutionaries, Trotsky for the more radical Mensheviks, and Lenin for the hard-line Bolshevik 'dictatorship of the proletariat'. Power was to pass from one to the other of them, in that

Tsarevich Alexis

The first demonstration in Petrograd, in front of the monument to Alexander III, in March 1917. Already red flags and revolutionary inscriptions can be seen

order. But by 1917 two crucial things had changed: the Duma existed, and the loyal army on which Tsardom depended had been largely destroyed by the war and its place taken by conscripted and disillusioned peasants.

Great crowds of workers and troops converged on the Duma, looking for leadership, and Rodzianko telephoned to Stavka imploring Nicholas to form a representative government. Still blind to reality, Nicholas remarked 'that fat fool Rodzianko has sent me some more rubbish', and refused to answer. The next day the Tsar's Council of Ministers in Petrograd was dispersed and a temporary committee of government was formed by the Duma, with Rodzianko as chairman. Simultaneously, a Petrograd Workers' and Soldiers' Soviet was set up alongside the Duma in the Tauride Palace to represent the revolutionary forces from the factories and the army, and to share power – uneasily from the first – with Rodzianko's committee.

Rodzianko tried to make arrangements for the Tsar's family to be moved to safety from the palace at Tsarskoe Selo, but Alexandra refused to leave. For one thing, her children were down with measles; for another, she still failed to understand what was happening. 'I'll never believe in the possibility of revolution,' she said that morning. 'I'm sure the trouble is confined to Petrograd.' On that same day, 13 March, Nicholas decided to return to Tsarskoe Selo, and left Stavka in the Imperial train. His own assessment of the situation was probably the same as Alix's.

The 'trouble', however, was not confined to Petrograd: the conflicting voices in the Tauride Palace spoke for huge masses across Russia. To the horrors and hardships of the war and the corruption and inefficiency of Imperial government a third cause of revolt had been growing – a growing political awareness throughout the country. Russian society had never been quite

A demonstration in front of the Winter Palace in Petrograd

the same since 1905; in spite of repression there had been some freedom of speech and of the press, and not only the liberals but also the defeated parties of the left had remained active and spread their influence in men's minds. While Lenin was an apparently forgotten exile and his following at home small, there were still Bolsheviks in Russia, and socialist propaganda – carried out by them and the Mensheviks and Socialist Revolutionaries – had a very considerable effect, particularly in the army. From early March unit after unit refused to obey officers, and sometimes shot them, and they were supported not only by organised labour in the factories of many cities but also by the railway and telegraph workers on whom the whole communications system of the Russian Empire depended. There was also a complete collapse of law and order: not only in Petrograd were the police torn to pieces.

On 14 March the Petrograd Soviet issued Army Order Number One, which handed over control of all military units to soldiers' committees. At the same time Rodzianko's Duma committee – of which Milyukov was the leading member – was trying desperately to establish its own authority, and to keep the revolution within bounds acceptable to liberal society. As in 1905, the Russian liberals were riding a tiger which would eventually eat them. Milyukov's aims were to force Nicholas to abdicate in favour of the Tsarevich, and to create the constitutional monarchy of which he had always dreamed, although popular opinion was already demanding greater reforms than that.

Rodzianko telegraphed General Alexeyev at Stavka, asking the Army Staff to press Nicholas to abdicate, and Alexeyev immediately obtained messages from all Army commanders begging the Tsar to stand down. Nicholas's own train was stopped by rebellious troops and railway workers and diverted to Northern Army Headquarters at Pskov, where General Ruzsky handed him the message from the Army commanders. It was probably at this moment that Nicholas admitted defeat and the calm dignity of doom descended on him. He made Ruzsky wire to Rodzianko, offering a constitution, but Rodzianko replied in great agitation: 'His majesty and yourself apparently are unable to understand what is happening . . . I am hanging by a thread myself. Power is slipping from my hands. The measures you propose are too late. The time for them is gone. There is no return.' Already two members of the Duma were on their way to

Pskov to demand the Tsar's abdication. By the time they arrived, Nicholas had made up his mind to assign the throne to his younger brother, the Grand Duke Michael, rather than to the Tsarevich: the love and humanity which Nicky reserved for his family circle prevented him from handing on the Romanov burden to the ailing Alexis. 'You will understand a father's feelings,' he said.

The paradox of Nicholas II is that he would almost certainly have been happier with the liberal democracy which he had always feared. If, as everyone had been saying for twenty years, Russia was an autocracy without an autocrat, it is equally true that Nicholas was a potential constitutional monarch without a constitution. Had he been born to the English throne, he could well have become an adequate and popular king (like his cousin George V whom he much resembled), from whom no major political initiative was required. As it was, the limits of his understanding made him incapable of fulfilling one role or accepting the other; the tragedy of the Romanovs, like most tragedies, was as much as anything the result of a failure of imagination. Although incapable of real autocracy, Nicholas had been brought up to regard it as his privilege and duty, had come to it reluctantly, carried it ineffectually, and put it down with relief. Those who witnessed his abdication, in the train at Pskov, were impressed by his calmness and courtesy, and from then on he seems to have behaved impeccably. The most retiring of the Romanovs withdrew into his own private family life. He was no longer important.

In Petrograd events were careering away from the Duma committee's control. Smoke from burning buildings rose above the frozen city and there were outbursts of firing. 'Great lorries rushed past crowded with revolutionary soldiers with fixed and pointed bayonets, bellowing as they went by.'[1] The Tauride Palace overflowed with 'large crowds of workers and soldiers, carrying red banners and singing the *Marseillaise*. . . . They surged through the corridors and chambers and engulfed the parliament. . . . There were soldiers, tall and hot in their rough wool uniforms; students shouting exultantly; and here and there a few grey-bearded old men, just released from prison, their knees trembling, their eyes shining.'[2]

The whole business was amateurish, exuberant, and accomplished with surprisingly little bloodshed, yet fateful. Among the crowd the revolutionary soviets were already bidding for power against the more conservative Duma leadership.

Work is almost impossible; people come in from all sides to beg advice of the members. Kerensky is calling for Rodzianko; officers are being killed and something must be done at once. Some of the invaders almost attack Rodzianko, who exclaims: 'What a rabble!' They are accusing him of being a capitalist. He thumps on a table and shouts: 'Take my shirt, if you want, but save Russia!'[3]

In the middle of it all Milyukov sat, grey and untiring, trying to draw up a constitution.

After much debate a Provisional Government was formed under the liberal *zemstvo* leader Prince Lvov, with Milyukov as Foreign Minister and Kerensky as Minister of Justice. When the delegates from Pskov returned to Petrograd, Rodzianko and members of the new government met Grand Duke Michael in private. A fragile, pleasure-loving young man, Michael was not at all sure that he wanted to take the crown. Milyukov implored him to but Kerensky, representing the socialists, wanted an end to monarchy, and so did several others. Finally, Michael declined the throne, and Russia was suddenly a republic.

The new government was mainly Liberal and pledged to an early general election and the creation of a new, completely democratic parliament – the Constituent Assembly which Milyukov had been advocating for a quarter of a century. But there was no administration, no certainty, no security. 'All Russia is camping out,' Kerensky said. Even in this moment of greatest achievement, the Liberals failed, for the country was still swinging left, and within the government the main influence passed from Milyukov's hands into those of Kerensky.

Kerensky was thirty-six, not tall or striking in looks, except for the intense expression of his eyes, but full of nervous energy, with a keen brain and a marvellous gift of oratory. 'He spoke decisively, authoritatively, as one who had not lost his head. . . . He seemed to grow every minute.'[4] It was he who, in the first days of revolution, flashed like a meteor between the Duma and Soviet, holding them together; he who swayed the crowds outside the Tauride Palace; he who marched the arrested Protopopov through the building shouting, 'Don't dare touch that man!'; he who first proclaimed, 'The Imperial Duma does not shed blood'.

There was undoubtedly something of megalomania in Kerensky's make-up, yet for all his vanity and histrionics he stood for humane and constitutional socialism, and was the one man of his time who could have led Russia to it. He was 'one of those who can dance on a marsh',[5] but the Socialist Revolutionaries had never had much organisation, and Kerensky had none on which to build. He tried to do everything himself, by oratory and conciliation, moving adroitly from one firm foothold to the next, until finally there was nowhere left to stand.

By the end of March the revolution had lost some of its first impetus and the Provisional Government settled down to churning out legislation, continually prodded by the Petrograd Soviet, while the country floundered in confusion. As Minister of Justice, Kerensky set up the inevitable inquisition of the leaders of the old régime, beginning with the Tsar and Tsarina, but his methods were both personal and merciful. He abolished capital punishment and told the Moscow Soviet, 'I will not be the Marat of the Russian Revolution,' adding incautiously, 'I will take the Tsar to Murmansk myself'.

The Provisional Government had already asked Britain to give the Imperial family asylum, and arrangements were made to send a British warship to collect them from Murmansk, while Wilhelm's government in Berlin agreed to give the ship unmolested passage. Meanwhile Nicholas had returned under arrest to Tsarskoe Selo, and he and Alix were interrogated there by Kerensky. Nothing much came out of the interviews except an unexpected mutual regard. Kerensky was surprised by Nicholas's 'unassuming manner and complete absence of pose', and reported both the Tsar and Tsarina innocent of treason, while Nicholas came to the conclusion that Kerensky was 'not a bad sort. He is a good fellow. One can talk to him. He is a man who loves Russia.' Kerensky promised that the government would protect the Imperial family and eventually send them to safety; but the Petrograd Soviet forbade their removal to Murmansk and the British offer was later withdrawn. The brief honeymoon was over: the revolution was entering upon darker ways.

Russia was still at war with Germany, although the Germans

had made no move on the Eastern Front since the revolution started. Wilhelm's government continued to hope that the revolutionaries would ask for peace, but the Provisional Government, under pressure from the Western allies, decided to go on fighting. The United States declared war on Germany in April and offered a large loan in return for a new Russian offensive. Feeling desperately in need of support from the Western democracies, the Provisional Government agreed; but the result was fatal to its own chances and to Kerensky's.

Years of war and weeks of agitation had destroyed the morale of most of the Russian army. Although its officers were still prepared to fight, the troops – like most people in Russia – wanted to go home and live in peace and enjoy the benefits of the revolution. 'The soldiers did not want to fight any more,' General Brusilov wrote. 'The officer at once became an enemy in the soldier's mind, for he demanded continuance of the war; and in the soldiers' eyes represented the type of master in military uniform.' Within two months of Army Order Number One, two million soldiers had deserted. 'To the average Russian peasant, his country was the hovel on the Volga, or perhaps in the Urals, where he happened to be born, and to which he thought the Germans could never penetrate.'[6] If the land was to be redistributed, he wanted to be there: he was tired and hungry, and Russia urgently needed food.

All this had occurred between the day Lenin read about the revolution by the Swiss lakeside and the day he sat in a train approaching the Finland Station of Petrograd. He was not, after all, forgotten: both wings of the Social Democratic party turned out to give him a tumultuous welcome. By the evening of 16 April large crowds were waiting at the station with red banners, military bands, armoured cars, searchlights and flowers. Lenin, expressionless, wearing a round cap, a magnificent bouquet in his hands, was led among cheers from the train to the former Imperial waiting-room, where the Menshevik leader of the Petrograd Soviet made a speech of welcome. At the end of it Lenin turned on his hosts and rent them, condemning the war and the Provisional Government, and the Mensheviks for supporting them. He demanded:

a decisive break with social-patriots, defencists and pacifists, both inside and outside Russia. This removed in advance any possibility of co-operation with Mensheviks and Socialist Revolutionaries as long as they adhered to their policy of giving support, however circumscribed, to the Russian war effort . . . Lenin drew a line of continuity between the Paris Commune in 1871, the St Petersburg Soviet of 1905 and the existing Petrograd Soviet of Workers' and Soldiers' Deputies. This latter he called 'the germ cell of a workers' government'.[7]

He ended: 'Any day now the whole of European capitalism may crash. The Russian revolution accomplished by you has prepared the way and opened a new epoch.'

Lenin and his followers went on to Kschessinska's former villa, now stripped and used as Bolshevik headquarters, and argued out a policy which was soon to sweep across Russia in the slogan 'Peace, Land, all Power to the Soviets'. 'I hardly spoke to Ilyich that night,' Krupskaya wrote. 'There were really no words to express the experience.'[8] The Bolsheviks now stood alone as a political force, but their influence over the workers and soldiers, and even among the peasantry, grew prodigiously in the following weeks: by July they had nearly 200,000 members.

In May Trotsky returned from abroad and threw in his lot with Lenin, and in the same month Milyukov resigned from the Provisional Government and Kerensky was made Minister of War, with the task of putting the army back on the offensive. He went everywhere, cajoled the generals and harangued the men, and was always dramatic. 'It is easy to appeal to exhausted men to throw down their arms and go home, where a new life has begun,' he told them. 'But I summon you to battle, to feats of heroism. I summon you not to festivity but to death; to sacrifice yourselves to save your country!' The soldiers called him Little Napoleon and Joan of Arc, but by July the army was able to launch a moderately successful offensive against the Austrians.

In the battle of giants which now developed between Kerensky and Lenin, Kerensky seemed to be the more strongly placed. A Bolshevik rising in the capital in July was easily put down, Lenin fled to Finland and Trotsky was imprisoned. Kerensky became Prime Minister of a coalition government of eleven moderate socialists and seven liberals. But the German army, as usual, came to the rescue of the Austrians, and Russia's less than half-hearted troops suffered their last defeat. The exhausted military

Lenin addressing a crowd, with Trotsky standing beside the platform on the right of the photograph

force which had failed the Tsar now failed the Provisional Government. Stavka reported: 'The Army is simply a huge, weary, shabby and ill-fed mob of angry men united by their common thirst for peace and by common disappointment.' The front dissolved; not even Kerensky could charm this home-going flood.

In mid-August the government decided to send Citizen Nicholas Romanov and his family eastwards for safety, and Kerensky characteristically supervised their departure himself. At Tsarskoe Selo Nicholas and Alix and their children were living under house arrest in relative comfort, although exposed to insult and deprived of freedom. Alexandra remained, in Kerensky's words, 'proud, domineering, irreconcilable'. Nicholas adapted himself more easily, digging the garden and sawing wood (a curious pleasure, which he shared with Wilhelm), but, as one of their few remaining friends wrote, 'his face was covered with innumerable wrinkles, his hair was quite grey at the temples, and blue shadows encircled his eyes. He looked like an old man.'[9]. His hope lay in Kerensky.

Kerensky, as Minister of War in the Provisional Government, taking the salute

Kerensky chose Tobolsk, in Siberia, as their next stopping-place, because it was quiet, remote and on the way to Vladivostok, from where they might later leave the country. He ordered a train for the 'Japanese Red Cross Mission' and himself saw them on to it: Nicholas, Alix, their young son and four daughters, a few servants, including a doctor and the children's Swiss tutor, Gilliard, a military escort, a great deal of luggage and Alix's pet spaniel. 'I have no fear. We trust you,' Nicholas told him, and set off into the Siberian exile to which he had dispatched so many of his subjects. At Tobolsk they settled into the ex-Governor's house, closely guarded but not ill-treated, and waited and prayed.

Their prayers were not answered. In September pressure from the left forced Kerensky to form a new government; outbreaks of peasant violence followed the return home of the troops; established society, feeling the rot had gone far enough, looked around for a stronger man to stop it. On 7 September the Cossack General Kornilov sent troops against Petrograd and Kerensky appealed to the Soviets for help. Among the Soviet

The Tsar with his son and daughters in Tobolsk, where they were interned from September 1917 to April 1918

factions the Bolsheviks were by then dominant: Lenin's insistence, since 1903, on a disciplined and centralised party was at last justified – Bolshevik order, and the absolute simplicity and clarity of Lenin's aims, cut through the disorder and confusion of a stalling revolution. They recruited, from the factory areas, a kind of workers' vigilantes, armed them and called them the Red Guard. Together with the revolutionary soldiers they faced Kornilov's forces, and his counter-revolutionary troops faded away.

Red Guards in Petrograd, 1917

From then on Kerensky was virtually powerless. The Red Guard refused to hand in their arms and Trotsky, released from prison, began in secret to prepare a coup d'état. For several more weeks Kerensky tried, almost single-handed, to hold society in its old upright position while growing, elemental forces were struggling, in Lenin's words, to bring the bottom to the top. It was a remarkable effort. The head of the British mission remembers Kerensky's desperate appeal from the platform of the Bolshoy Theatre in Moscow:

He looked ill and tired. He drew himself up to his full height, as if calling up his last reserves of energy. Then, with an ever-increasing flow of words, he began to expound his gospel of suffering. Nothing that was worth having was achieved without suffering. Man himself was born into this world in suffering. The greatest of all revolutions in history had begun on the Cross of Calvary. Was it to be supposed that their own revolution was to be consolidated without suffering? . . . As he finished his peroration, he sank back exhausted into the arms of his aide-de-camp. Soldiers assisted him off the stage, while in a frenzy of hysteria the whole audience rose and cheered itself hoarse. . . . The speech had lasted for two hours. Its effect on Moscow and on the rest of Russia lasted exactly two days.[10]

At the beginning of November Lenin returned to Moscow and began to direct the policy behind Trotsky's revolutionary work.

'If we do not act now,' he said, 'history will not forgive us.' The Bolshevik-dominated Soviets now occupied the Smolny Institute, in a Petrograd suburb, and the real energy of the revolution was centred there, among scenes similar to those in the Tauride Palace in the early spring.

The Petrograd Soviet was meeting continuously at Smolny, a centre of storm, delegates falling down asleep on the floor and rising again to take part in the debate, Trotsky, Kamenev, Volodarsky speaking six, eight, twelve hours a day. . . . As night fell the great hall filled up with soldiers and workmen, a monstrous dun mass, deep-humming in a blue haze of smoke. . . . Martov tried to speak, but could not be heard. . . . Towards four in the morning I met Sorin in the outer hall, a rifle slung over his shoulder. 'We're moving!' said he, calmly, but with satisfaction. . . . Far over the still roofs westward came the sound of scattered rifle fire, where the *yunkers** were trying to open the bridges over the Neva, to prevent the factory workers and soldiers of the Vyborg quarter from joining the Soviet forces in the centre of the city; and the Kronstadt sailors were closing them again. . . . Behind us great Smolny, bright with lights, hummed like a gigantic hive.[11]

By 7 November Trotsky's forces controlled most of Petrograd and that evening, supported by the Soviet-manned cruiser

* Officer cadets.

Crowds in front of the University in Petrograd while a decree is read out

Trotsky's forces storm the Winter Palace

Aurora, they stormed the Winter Palace where the Provisional Government was in session. There was no real resistance; Kerensky escaped and his fellow ministers were arrested. The following night a Soviet Government was formed, with Lenin as President. The obdurate exile had triumphed: under his hand a red tide was to spread from the city which was to take his name, sweeping away the last remnants of Tsarist Russia, its old faith, its fragile liberalism, its dawning hopes of constitutional democracy; but by great effort, against bitter opposition and with an almost unimaginable renewal of suffering.

At Tobolsk, Nicholas heard the news from the capital with dismay. To him Lenin seemed only a scoundrel, a cheap traitor planted by the Germans. 'I then for the first time heard the Tsar regret his abdication,' Gilliard wrote. 'It now gave him pain to see that his renunciation had been in vain.' The Romanovs faced the Siberian winter and waited, in silent fear, for the Bolshevik commissars to come.

Chapter fourteen
All Fall Down

The Hapsburgs were the next to go. Few men can have inherited such a spectacularly bankrupt estate as Emperor Karl of Austria-Hungary, or put it into liquidation with such good intentions. He was totally opposed to the war and set himself 'to win back for my peoples the sorely-missed blessings of peace', to break the ties with Germany, and to transform the Hapsburg Empire into a federation of largely independent states. 'Dualism cannot be saved. Trialism is not just and anyway doesn't go far enough,' he said. 'The only solution is a truly federal one to give all the peoples a chance.'

He was a bright and likeable man of thirty, cheerful and kind, generous and perceptive, although without experience. He and his Italian wife Zita made a popular couple, even at a time when royal popularity was in so steep a decline, and were not without courage – but they came too late: Europe was no longer susceptible to imperial indulgence. Karl had already tried, in 1917, to reach agreement with France and had warned Wilhelm: 'We are fighting against a new enemy which is more dangerous than the Entente – against international revolution which finds its strongest ally in general starvation. . . . A quick finish to the war – even at the cost of heavy sacrifice – gives us a chance of confronting the oncoming upheaval with success.' Both these moves failed and by the beginning of 1918 the forces against him had

Emperor Karl and Empress Zita of Austria-Hungary in their coronation robes

become overwhelming. While the elegant routines of the great Schönbrunn palace in Vienna continued undisturbed, the Empire fell apart.

By 1918 the Austrian casualty lists rose to four million; the Imperial army in Italy, although reinforced from the Eastern Front, was being reduced to a rabble; there were critical shortages of food and munitions. The revolutionary influence of Russia gave new heart and impetus to the nationalist movements of Slavs, Poles, Czechs and Hungarians, and even within Austria itself demands for peace and a new order grew rapidly stronger – the Vienna cafés were empty of coffee and full of anarchy. Karl's Foreign Minister, Count Czernin, told Berlin: 'If the monarchs of the Central Powers are not able to conclude peace during the next few months, the peoples will go over their heads and the waves of the revolutionary flood will sweep away everything for which our brothers and sons are still fighting and dying.' But the German government did not believe it.

Germany, in the grip of a military dictatorship which continued to demand total victory, survived the winter not only unbroken but apparently strengthened by the collapse of Russian resistance. The prospect of peace with the new Soviet government brought with it the release of German forces from the east and hopes of vast new supplies from the captured Ukraine. Negotiations, however, dragged on through January and February and into March, at Brest Litovsk in Poland, with Trotsky parrying the German demands: 'a clever and very dangerous adversary,' Count Czernin called him, 'with a swiftness and adroitness in retort which I have rarely seen.'

Peace with Russia was finally signed on 3 March 1918, and Germany, victorious in the east, threw her whole strength against the west, binding Austria to her in a new treaty signed at Spa in May in spite of all Karl's objections. Spa, in Belgium, was now the headquarters of the German High Command and there Hindenburg and Ludendorff, with Wilhelm's connivance, prepared their great and final onslaught.

The campaign which followed was known as 'the Kaiser's battle' and the whole war 'the Kaiser's War'. Yet Wilhelm, regarded as 'the embodiment of all the real and invented atrocities of this war'[1] was simply the prisoner of his own misplaced enthusiasm and had sold out his imperial powers to the generals in exactly the way that Fritz and Vicky had feared.

Wilhelm II visits an aviation camp

Erratic and directionless, sometimes sensible and sometimes silly, he was increasingly ignored: 'The Kaiser was so pitifully inadequate that he verges on tragedy'.[2] Nevertheless, his was officially the voice of Germany, and one which enemies and friends heard with alarm. As ever Germany was in two minds: the militaristic élite wanted an eventual peace which guaranteed large increases in German territory, power and prestige; the progressive civilian leadership wanted peace at once, without gains, and a new, democratic form of government.

When the military situation was good, Wilhelm spoke up for the soldiers; at times of reverse and unrest he promised moderation and reform; but as in fact he always in the end deferred to the High Command, little account was taken of him. He rarely appeared in public, and complained, 'Not a soul is grateful to me'. The nature of his failure was understood well enough by the Empress Zita. 'If we had a friend in Germany it was the Emperor William,' she said. 'But he was completely under the thumb of his generals. This, I think was largely because he was such a dreamer. He believed in his dreams and one of them, unfortunately, was that of final victory.'

In March 1918 Wilhelm was at Spa with Hindenburg and Ludendorff, whom he called the Siamese Twins – the Kaiser retained, on his better days, an irascible humour which made

Wilhelm II at the front with General von Moltke, October 1914

him at the same time engaging and insufferable, but he also indulged in 'very disagreeable outbursts of megalomania, which always ensue when things are going well for us,' as Müller, one of his aides, noticed. He was tolerated at Headquarters because imperialism required an emperor and there was no visible alternative to him. The Crown Prince, 'Little Willy', was a dissolute and disagreeable young man whom few relished. 'Be careful not to shoot the Kaiser,' people said, 'or we'll get something much worse'; and Hindenburg, at least, had an old-fashioned loyalty to his sovereign.

The battle-plan, as usual, was Ludendorff's. Germany's Western Front troops, reinforced from the east, were to sweep the British army into the English Channel and dispatch France before American forces could become effective in Europe. Austria, meanwhile, was to hold off the Italians and stand guard in the Balkans. Like the Schlieffen Plan, it was an inspired gamble, and like the Schlieffen Plan it failed. The first attack, in the St Quentin sector of the British line, was an initial success. Outnumbering the British three to one, the Germans captured 90,000 men, 1300 guns and two million bottles of whisky. An excited Wilhelm shouted from his train to a railway guard, 'The battle is won – the English have been utterly defeated.' But the Allied line, although bent, was unbroken, and in May five reserve British divisions halted Ludendorff's major offensive at Soisson.

In July the last and heaviest German attack was launched against Rheims. The French commander, Marshal Foch, admitted, 'If the German offensive at Rheims succeeds, the Germans have won the war.' Germany, however, was no longer as strong as its High Command thought. In the face of desperate resistance, the morale of army and people began to ebb; while victory had seemed possible they were willing to endure appalling hardship, but now they felt that blood was being spilt for nothing. Reinforced by half a million American field troops, the Allies stopped the advance on Rheims and counter-attacked, using tanks in large numbers for the first time. The Germans broke. Wilhelm could not understand it. 'It's very strange,' he noted, 'that our men cannot get used to tanks.'

Ludendorff also broke. An emotional man and a far-sighted strategist, he saw in the defeat the ultimate destruction of the whole German military machine. He flew into rages, tried to resign and later collapsed, while Hindenburg stolidly withdrew

The house at Ekaterinburg where the Imperial family were assassinated

the German Western Front to defensive positions and held out for an honourable peace. 'Things can't go on like this indefinitely and we must find a way to end it,' Wilhelm acknowledged; but he had no idea what to do.

He retired to his castle at Wilhelmshole where the Empress, Dona, was ill, and there heard the horrifying news from Russia – that ex-Tsar Nicholas and his family had been executed by the Bolsheviks at Ekaterinburg in the Urals. The colour of his fantasies changed. He could not sleep. 'Mocking visions of his English and Russian relatives and all the Ministers and Generals of his own reign filed before him.'[3] He began to look older. He was attacked by sciatica and walked with a stick. While the carnage on the Western Front continued and the German line was gradually pushed back, he suffered a sort of paralysis of will and a short physical breakdown. Stripped of a lifetime of illusion, he retreated into a deeper pretence that what was occurring did not touch him. Müller wrote, 'We behave here as though nothing had happened.'

On 25 September Bulgaria opted out of the war. A small ally, she had all the same linked the Central Powers with Turkey, and her defection left the Balkans open to the Entente: Turkey was now isolated and bound to collapse, and Austria vulnerable to an attack on a new front which she was in no state to resist. Karl's fears had been justified – his Empire was breaking up. 'In jumping clear of us,' it was said in Berlin, 'Bulgaria has knocked the bottom out of the barrel.'

In Vienna a Czech spokesman had already declared publicly,

'We regard Austria as a centuries-old crime against humanity', and in August Britain recognised Czechoslovakia as an 'Allied nation'. On 16 October Karl published his 'Peoples' Manifesto', which promised a federation of independent states, but even so loose a hold was no longer tolerable; the initiative had passed out of his hands. In October an independent Czechoslovakian republic was proclaimed in Prague, the Hungarians, Slavs and Poles were rushing towards their own freedom, and the parliament in Vienna formed itself into a Provisional National Assembly. On 27 October Karl wrote to Wilhelm that Austria had no alternative but to stop fighting and make peace. From then on Germany would be without friends. Two nights later Wilhelm left home for ever, to rejoin Army Headquarters at Spa.

Germany's ambition had now shrunk to securing an armistice before her army was decimated and the Fatherland invaded. Ludendorff had recovered and become as choleric a protagonist of instant peace as he had been of continued war, and Hindenburg announced, 'To avoid further sacrifices, His Majesty has been advised to break off the battle.' A new Chancellor, Prince Max of Baden, was appointed to form a more popular government and immediately opened peace negotiations with the Western Allies, who had no intention of leaving a military empire intact to fight another day. Their reply was based on the Fourteen Points drawn up by President Wilson of the United States, which stipulated that if they were to deal with 'military leaders and monarchical autocracy' they must demand 'not peace negotiations but surrender'.

The only prudent response to this was to transfer power from the Kaiser and his commanders to a Chancellor responsible to a democratic German parliament, and arrangements were put in hand for this by Max of Baden, who was an enlightened Prince though somewhat incapacitated by influenza. The inference that Wilhelm himself would have to go was lost on no one, and he himself was roused from his lethargy by the very thought of it. 'A descendant of Frederick the Great does not abdicate,' he objected, but the boast had a hollow ring; in the eyes of his subjects, he stood between them and peace. Princess Blücher wrote: 'As for the mood of the people the heroic attitude has completely disappeared. Now one sees faces like masks, blue with cold and drawn by hunger.' They were not prepared to go through another winter of war.

Wilhelm II in July 1917

In the past year the revolutionary wing of the German Socialist party had made the sort of progress which Lenin had hoped for. Lenin had always believed that the workers would rise in all belligerent countries and unite in a peaceful fraternity of world communism; such risings had already started in Austria, and in Germany were obviously imminent. Against that, the German parliament, frustrated for generations, was suddenly in a powerful position. It seems likely that virtually all its members – conservatives, liberals and democratic socialists – would have accepted a constitutional monarchy with Wilhelm's grandson as the monarch and a democratically elected Regent. But Wilhelm would not abdicate. At Army Headquarters he felt safe, and when Ludendorff asked impatiently when the new government was to be formed the Kaiser replied tartly, 'I am not a conjurer'. Late in October Ludendorff was dismissed and his place given to General Gröner, the military railway chief who had always been kind to his sovereign. At Spa the Army Headquarters were quartered, comically enough, in the *Hotel Britannique,* and Wilhelm in a large house nearby, where he remained into the first week of November, agitated and intransigent, while the killing on the Western front went on.

The stalemate was broken by revolution. On 1 November the sailors of the Imperial Navy at Kiel mutinied and took over the city. By the seventh most cities in Germany were in the hands of revolutionaries and the Social Democrats in the capital were demanding the Kaiser's immediate abdication. Agonised telephone appeals came from Prince Max and others in Berlin, but Wilhelm replied, 'I have no intention of quitting the throne because of a few hundred Jews and a thousand workmen'. Splendidly and unrealistically foolish to the last, he decided to march on the revolutionaries at the head of his troops, and then – joining hands with England and Japan – 'fling the Americans out of Europe'; but the Army commanders were unenthusiastic. Gröner realised that the German army was prepared to fight for its Kaiser no longer, against the Allies or anyone else, and the following day he convinced Hindenburg.

On 9 November Wilhelm met his generals for the last time, in the chilly garden room of his Spa house. 'Sire, you no longer have an army,' Gröner told him. 'The army will march home in peace and order under its leaders and commanding generals, but not under the command of Your Majesty, for it no longer stands behind Your Majesty.' Hindenburg wept, but could offer no comfort. A few minutes later a message arrived from Berlin: 'All troops deserted – completely out of hand.'

Wilhelm went out into the damp, autumnal garden to think about it. 'I have lived for sixty years and spent thirty of them on the throne,' he had recently said. 'Who is to take my place?' He could see nothing ahead but defeat, a republic and the end of his dynasty. Those there remembered him haggard and trembling. He went back into the house and agreed to abdicate. The news was immediately telephoned to Prince Max in Berlin, and at the last moment Wilhelm added that, although no longer German Emperor, he would remain King of Prussia; but this suggestion was lost in the confusion.

That evening arrangements were made to smuggle the ex-Kaiser into Holland. Hindenburg particularly was afraid of his former sovereign suffering the fate of the Tsar, and the Dutch border was only twenty miles away. Wilhelm wrote to the Crown Prince, 'Dear Boy – I have decided, after a severe struggle, to leave', and signed it, 'Your stricken father'.

On the same evening, ministers from the new Austrian Government visited the Emperor Karl in the Schönbrunn palace in

Vienna with a document renouncing his rule. He signed it in one of the Chinese rooms, and went to pray. He had concluded peace with the Allies on 4 November and since then had been Emperor only in name; Vienna was full of hysterical crowds and the Government in the hands of a socialist Chancellor, Dr Karl Renner.

It was doubtful whether the Imperial family would be allowed to leave; but two nights later Renner arrived at Schönbrunn with two cars and is alleged to have said, 'Herr Hapsburg, the taxi is waiting'. With this superb curtain-line possibly ringing in their ears the last generation of the seven-hundred-year-old Hapsburg dynasty were driven to the comparative safety of Ackartsau castle, and from there took a train into Switzerland. They were lucky to escape with their lives.

By now more horrifying news had arrived from Russia. Gilliard, returning with White Russians to Ekaterinburg, found evidence which indicated that Nicholas, Alexandra and their children had been shot against a wall in the basement of the house in which they had been held prisoner since leaving Tobolsk, and that their bodies had been taken to a disused salt mine outside the town and there cut up and burnt, their bones dissolved in sulphuric acid and the remains thrown down the mine shaft. Among the charred pieces they found jewels, two belt buckles, some corsets, a set of false teeth, and what was thought to be one of the Tsarina's fingers. Most of the rest of the Imperial family suffered a similar doom; only the Dowager Empress Marie, her entourage and some lesser royalty managed to escape to England. Rasputin had been right.

On 10 November Wilhelm arrived at the Dutch frontier and surrendered his sword to the frontier guard. No one in Holland seemed to know what to do with him, but eventually a Count Goddard Bentinck offered him the hospitality of his home at Amerongen. 'Who is this Bentinck?' Wilhelm enquired. 'I don't think I know him.' On being assured that the Count was half English and not a mason, Wilhelm consented to go to Amerongen the next day.

The sad irony of the situation appears to have been lost on him. He had more than once said that, had he not been German Emperor, he would have been happy to be an English country squire. He had never intended to be a despot, only a beloved leader; he had not meant to precipitate a European war, least of all a war against his mother's country. One of his Chancellors wrote:

What Wilhelm II most desired was to see himself at the head of a glorious German fleet, starting out on a peaceful visit to England. The English sovereign, with his fleet, would meet the German Kaiser in Portsmouth. The two fleets would file past each other; the two monarchs – each wearing the naval uniform of the other's country – would then stand on the bridge of their flagships. Then, after they had embraced in the prescribed manner, a gala dinner with lovely speeches would be held in Cowes.

That England still existed, but not that Germany, that Russia, that Austria, that Europe. In the seventy years since the young Franz Josef had been thrust on to the Austrian throne, the entire continent had changed beyond recognition. Its harsh empires and gentle liberalism had been swept away together by revolution and war, and a new order was established which ensured, for better or worse, that its countries were no longer governed by the heirs of imperial families.

On the day Wilhelm arrived at the Goddard Bentinck residence, armistice was signed between Germany and the Western Allies, and the war which had cost three empires and over ten million human lives ended. Wilhelm appeared unmoved: as they drove through the rain into the courtyard of his new home, he is reputed to have said to his host, 'Now for a cup of really good English tea.'

Epilogue

Wilhelm lived on in exile until the middle of the Second World War. He bought a small estate at Doorn, in Holland, and lived very much of the life of an English country gentleman, busy with his wood-chopping, his dogs and his memoirs. His wife, Dona, died in 1921, and eighteen months later he married another German princess, Hermine of Schönaich-Carolath. Although Hermine was more than twenty-five years younger than him, their marriage was apparently a happy one. With the strains of being an Emperor irrevocably ended, he mellowed; his grand-children remembered him as a kindly old man, and his Dutch hosts respected him as 'a great gentleman'. Before the end of his life there was even a tenuous rapprochment with England: in 1938, after Neville Chamberlain's flight to Munich, the ex-Kaiser wrote to Queen Mary, and on his eightieth birthday he received congratulatory telegrams from the British royal family. When Hitler's armies invaded Holland he was offered refuge in England, but declined. He died in June 1941 and was buried at Doorn. His son, 'Little Willie', died in 1951.

His Russian relations had a harsher fate. Whatever doubt there may be concerning the deaths of Nicholas and his family, there is none about the murder of the Grand Duchess Ella, Alix's elder sister, who, with other victims, was thrown alive down a mineshaft into which hand grenades were hurled; nor of Grand Duke Michael, Nicholas's younger brother, who was shot a few days before the Ekaterinburg incident. The ex-Tsar's

The ex-Kaiser feeds his ducks at Doorn

mother, the Dowager Duchess Marie, left the Crimea on board a British battleship before the Red Army arrived; she returned later to her native Denmark and died there in 1928, apparently unshaken in her belief that Nicholas and his family were still alive. The Grand Duke Nicholas left with her and died in 1929 in Antibes, where he was given a military funeral; but Alexeyev, Kornilov and other senior commanders of the former Imperial army perished in the holacaust of the Russian civil war.

By the end of 1920 the Red Army, under Trotsky's hand, had swept the last of the White counter-revolutionary forces out of Russia. The revolution, which had started with little bloodshed, only succeeded at a cost of death and misery greater even than the Russians had suffered in the Great War. Lenin's government emerged secure, with Moscow as the capital of the Soviet Union; but many politicians of other parties disappeared in the years of post-war terror. Protopopov, among others, was tried and executed. Rodzianko fled and died in poverty in Belgrade in 1924; Milyukov outlived him, more comfortably, by ten years – a historian in exile. Kerensky made one attempt to return to

Petrograd, but was dissuaded by friends and smuggled out of the country, to live nearly another fifty years in exile, always hoping to return, and writing and lecturing endlessly – mainly about the half year when he stood at the pinnacle of power. He died in the United States in his late eighties.

Lenin himself did not long outlast the revolution. He survived an assassination attempt in 1919, and he and Krupskaya lived in a simple apartment in the Kremlin until 1924, when he died after a series of strokes. As he lay dying he said sadly to Krupskaya, 'They say Martov is dying too'. Martov had gone with a Menshevik delegation to Berlin and never returned. Trotsky, who had hoped to succeed Lenin, was ousted by Stalin, at whose instigation he was murdered in 1940.

All through the 1920s émigrés from the old régimes eked out their lives in Paris, London, New York and other havens, living on their wits and jewels and dreaming of a return to glory; but as Europe assumed its new shape their dreams faded. Of all the former Emperors, the only one with a real chance of regaining a throne was Karl of Austria. There was clearly no place for him in Vienna, but he had also been King of Hungary, and Hungary's constitutional future was by no means settled.

Karl remained in Switzerland from 1918 to 1921 with his wife Zita and their children – their seventh was born there and christened Rudolf. Karl began to suffer from heart attacks but still looked hopefully towards Budapest. Immediately after the war a communist Hungarian government was established under Bela Kun, but in November 1920 it was overthrown by Admiral Horthy, a former Imperial aide. Karl returned twice to Hungary – in the spring and autumn of 1921 – but was ejected by Horthy, the first time peacefully, the second after a small battle outside Budapest. In October 1921 Karl and Zita were taken into the custody of the Allies and sailed away down the Danube in the British monitor *Glow-worm*. In November they landed in Madeira, where they were joined by their children, and in April the following year Karl died there, of pneumonia. The House of Hapsburg – like the Houses of Romanov and Hohenzollern – passed into what Trotsky called 'the dustbin of history'.

Karl and his family in exile at Prangins in Switzerland

House of Hohenzollern   FREDERICK
WILHELM III
1770-1840
King of Prussia 1797
m. ———————
Louise of
Mecklenburg-Strelitz

┌ FREDERICK
│ WILHELM IV
│ 1795-1861
│
├ WILHELM I
│ 1797-1888
│ Emp. of Germany 1871
│ m. ———————
│ Augusta of Weimar
│
└ Charlotte
   m.
   Nicholas I
   (see below)

House of Windsor   VICTORIA
1819-1901
Queen of England 1837
m. ————————————————————
Albert of Saxe-Coburg-Gotha
1819-61

House of Romanov   NICHOLAS I
1796-1855
Tsar 1825
m. ——————————— ALEXANDER II
Charlotte of Prussia   1818-81
(see above)   m. ——————————————
                        Marie of Hesse-Darmstadt

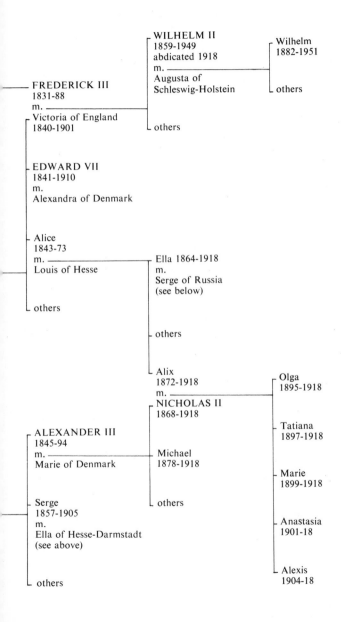

FREDERICK III
1831-88
m.
Victoria of England
1840-1901

WILHELM II
1859-1949
abdicated 1918
m.
Augusta of
Schleswig-Holstein

Wilhelm
1882-1951

others

others

EDWARD VII
1841-1910
m.
Alexandra of Denmark

Alice
1843-73
m.
Louis of Hesse

others

Ella 1864-1918
m.
Serge of Russia
(see below)

others

Alix
1872-1918
m.
NICHOLAS II
1868-1918

Olga
1895-1918

Tatiana
1897-1918

Marie
1899-1918

Anastasia
1901-18

Alexis
1904-18

ALEXANDER III
1845-94
m.
Marie of Denmark

Michael
1878-1918

others

Serge
1857-1905
m.
Ella of Hesse-Darmstadt
(see above)

others

House of Hapsburg

FRANCIS II ——————
1768-1835
Emp. of Austria 1792

┌ FERDINAND
│ 1793-1875
│ abdicated 1848
│
├ Franz Karl Josef
│ m. ——————————————
│ Sophie of Bavaria
│
│
└ Marie Louise
  m.
  Napoleon I

Chronology

1837 Victoria succeeds to English throne.
1840 Marriage of Queen Victoria and Prince Albert.
1848 'Year of Revolution': Franz Josef succeeds to Austrian throne.
      Louis Napoleon elected President of France.
1849 Suppression of Italy and Hungary by Austria.
1852 Napoleon III proclaimed French Emperor.
1854 Outbreak of Crimean War.
      Marriage of Emperor Franz Josef and Elizabeth of Bavaria.

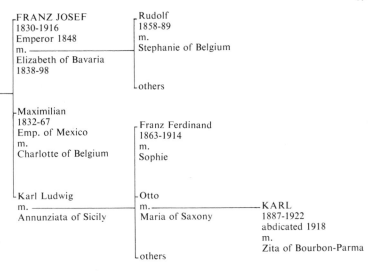

FRANZ JOSEF
1830-1916
Emperor 1848
m. ───────
Elizabeth of Bavaria
1838-98

Rudolf
1858-89
m.
Stephanie of Belgium

others

Maximilian
1832-67
Emp. of Mexico
m.
Charlotte of Belgium

Franz Ferdinand
1863-1914
m.
Sophie

Karl Ludwig
m. ───────
Annunziata of Sicily

Otto
m. ───────
Maria of Saxony

KARL
1887-1922
abdicated 1918
m.
Zita of Bourbon-Parma

others

1855   Alexander II succeeds to Russian throne.
1858   Marriage of Prince Frederick William of Prussia and Princess
        Victoria of England.
       Birth of Crown Prince Rudolf of Austria.
1859   Austrian defeat in Italy.
       Birth of Prince William of Prussia.
1861   William I succeeds to Prussian throne.
       Liberation of Russian serfs by Tsar Alexander II.
       Albert Prince Consort dies.
1862   Bismarck becomes Minister-President of Prussia.
1866   Austro-Prussian War.
1867   Dual Monarchy of Austria-Hungary.
       Great Exhibition at Paris.
       Karl Marx publishes Vol. I of 'Das Kapital'.
1868   Birth of Prince Nicholas of Russia.
1870   Birth of Lenin.
       Outbreak of Franco-Prussian War.
       Fall of Napoleon III.
1871   William I proclaimed German Emperor.
       Bismarck created German Chancellor.
       Paris Commune.
1878   Congress of Berlin.
1881   Revival of Three Emperors' League.
       Marriage of Prince William of Prussia and Augusta of
        Schleswig-Holstein.

1881   Assassination of Tsar Alexander II.
        Alexander III succeeds to Russian throne.
        Birth of Kerensky.
1883   Death of Karl Marx.
1884   Marriage of Grand Duke Serge of Russia and Ella of
           Hesse-Darmstadt.
1887   Alexander Ulyanov executed.
        Re-insurance Treaty between Germany and Russia.
1888   Deaths of Kaisers William I and Frederick III of Germany.
        William II succeeds to German throne.
1889   Death of Crown Prince Rudolf of Austria-Hungary.
1890   Fall of Bismarck.
1891   Triple Alliance of Germany, Austria and Italy.
1892   Russian-French treaty.
1893   Lenin arrives in St Petersburg.
1894   Death of Tsar Alexander III.
        Nicholas II succeeds to Russian throne and marries Alix of
           Hesse-Darmstadt.
1895   Milyukov exiled from Moscow.
        Lenin arrested.
1898   Marriage of Lenin and Krupskaya in Siberia.
        Russian Workers' Social Democratic Party formed.
        Assassination of Empress Elizabeth of Austria-Hungary.
        First German Navy Law.
1899   Kerensky arrives in St Petersburg.
1900   Plehve appointed Russian Minister of Interior.
1901   Death of Queen Victoria.
        Edward VII succeeds to English throne.
        Russian Social Revolutionary Terrorist Organisation formed.
        Death of Empress Victoria of Germany.
1902   Lenin and Trotsky meet in London.
1903   Russian Social Democratic Party Congress in London.
        Witte resigns from Tsar's ministry.
        Rasputin arrives in St Petersburg.
1904   Entente Cordiale between Britain and France.
        Outbreak of Russo-Japanese War.
        Plehve assassinated.
        Birth of Tsarevich Alexis.
1905   'Bloody Sunday' in St Petersburg.
        Assassination of Grand Duke Serge of Russia.
        Russian defeat in Far East.
        Revolt in Russia: Trotsky returns to St Petersburg.
        End of Russo-Japanese War.
        St Petersburg Soviet: Lenin returns to Russia.
        Witte appointed Russian First Minister.

1905   Tsar Nicholas issues October Manifesto.
1906   Suppression of revolt in Russia: Lenin and Trotsky return to
        exile.
        Witte dismissed.
        Opening of first Russian Duma.
        Stolypin appointed Russian First Minister.
1907   Russia joins Entente Cordiale.
1908   Austria annexes Bosnia.
1911   Stolypin assassinated.
        Death of King Edward VII.
        George V succeeds to English throne.
1914   Assassination of Archduke Franz Ferdinand of Austria-Hungary.
        Outbreak of Great War.
        Russian army defeated at Tannenburg.
        German army fails to reach Paris.
1915   Russian victory against Austria-Hungary.
        Italy declares war against Austria-Hungary.
        Successful German offensive against Russia.
        British and French defeated at Dardanelles.
        Tsar Nicholas II becomes C.-in-C. Russian forces.
        German government approaches Lenin.
1916   Russia and Austria suffer major defeats.
        Hindenburg appointed Chief of German General Staff.
        Death of Emperor Franz Josef.
        Karl I succeeds to throne of Austria-Hungary.
        Rasputin murdered.
1917   Germany opens unrestricted U-boat warfare.
        Revolution in Russia.
        Tsar Nicholas II abdicates: Provisional Russian Government
            formed.
        United States enters war against Germany.
        Lenin returns to Petrograd.
        Russian Imperial family moved to Siberia.
        Russian Provisional Government overthrown by Bolsheviks.
1918   Russo-German peace treaty signed at Brest-Litovsk.
        German defeat on Western Front.
        Nicholas and other members of Russian Imperial family
            murdered.
        Austrian army defeated in Italy.
        Hungary and Czechoslovakia cede from Austrian Empire.
        Armistice signed between Austria and Allies.
        Revolt in Germany.
        Emperor Karl of Austria abdicated.
        Abdication of Kaiser Wilhelm II.
        General armistice signed.

Notes

Chapter one

1 Anthony Wood, *Europe 1815–1945*.
2 Edward Crankshaw, *The Hapsburgs*.
3 Joseph Redlich, *Emperor Francis Joseph of Austria*.
4 Crankshaw, *op. cit.*

Chapter two

1 Theo Aronson, *The Kaisers*.

Chapter three

1 H. Bolitho, ed., *Later Letters of Lady Augusta Stanley*.

Chapter four

1 Aronson, *op. cit.*
2 Daphne Bennett, *Vicky*.

Chapter five

1 Aronson, *op. cit.*
2 Michael Balfour, *The Kaiser and his times*.

Chapter six

1 Crankshaw, *op. cit.*
2 Count Kalnoky, memorandum of January 1886.

Chapter eight

1 Nadezhda Krupskaya, *Memories of Lenin*.
2 Robert Payne, *The life and death of Lenin*.
3 Krupskaya, *op. cit.*
4 *Ibid.*

5 John Reed, *Ten days that shook the world.*
6 R. H. Bruce Lockhart, *Memoirs of a British agent.*
7 Alexander Kerensky, *The Kerensky memoirs.*
8 *Ibid.*
9 Richard Charques, *The twilight of Imperial Russia.*

Chapter nine
1 Charques, *op. cit.*

Chapter ten
1 Harold Nicolson, *Lord Carnock.*

Chapter eleven
1 Bernard Pares, *The fall of the Russian monarchy.*
2 *Ibid.*

Chapter twelve
1 Winston Churchill, *The world crisis.*
2 Pares, *op. cit.*
3 *Ibid.*
4 M. V. Rodzianko, *The reign of Rasputin.*
5 Balfour, *op. cit.*
6 *Ibid.*
7 Krupskaya, *op. cit.*
8 Alan Moorehead, *The Russian revolution.*
9 *Ibid.*
10 Churchill, *op. cit.*

Chapter thirteen
1 Pares, *op. cit.*
2 R. K. Massie, *Nicholas and Alexandra.*
3 Pares, *op. cit.*
4 V. V. Shulgin, *Days.*
5 *Ibid.*
6 Alfred Knox, *With the Russian army, 1914–17.*
7 Lionel Kochan, *Russia in revolution.*
8 Krupskaya, *op. cit.*
9 Lili Dehn, *The real Tsaritsa.*
10 Lockhart, *op. cit.*
11 Reed, *op. cit.*

Chapter fourteen
1 Prince Ernest zu Hohenlohe, in a letter.
2 Virginia Cowles, *The Kaiser.*
3 Balfour, *op. cit.*

Bibliography

The following books may be useful to the reader who would like to know more.

General books
BALDICK, R., *The Siege of Paris* (Batsford, 1964).
CHURCHILL, Sir Winston, *The world crisis,* 6 vols (Butterworth, 1929–31); n.e. 2 vols (New American Library, 1968).
DUFF, D., *Hessian tapestry* (Muller, 1967).
LONGFORD, Lady Elizabeth, *Victoria R. I* (Weidenfeld and Nicolson, 1964; Pan Books, 1966).
MAGNUS, Sir Philip, *King Edward VII* (John Murray, 1964).
MAUROIS, A., *King Edward VII and his times* (Cassell, 1949).
STRACHEY, L., *Queen Victoria* (Chatto and Windus, 1921; Collins, n.e. 1958; Penguin Books, n.e. 1971).
VICTORIA, Queen of England, *Letters* 3 series (John Murray).
  1st series, edited by A. C. Benson and Viscount Esher, 3 vols, 1907.
  2nd and 3rd series, edited by G. E. Buckle, 3 vols each, 1926–31.
VICTORIA, Queen of England, *Dearest child: letters between Queen Victoria and the Princess Royal, 1858–61,* edited by R. Fulford (Evans, 1964).
VICTORIA, Queen of England, *Dearest Mama* and *Your dear letter: letters between Queen Victoria and the Crown Princess of Prussia,* edited by R. Fulford (Evans, 1968–71).
WILSON, E., *To the Finland station* (Macmillan, n.e. 1973).
WOOD, A., *Europe, 1815–1945* (Longman, 1964).

Austria

BARKELEY, R., *The road to Mayerling* (Macmillan, 1958).

BROOK-SHEPHERD, G., *The last Hapsburg* (Weidenfeld and Nicolson, 1968).

CASSELS, L., *Clash of generations* (John Murray, 1973).

CORTI, Count Egon, *Elizabeth, Empress of Austria* (Butterworth, 1936).

CRANKSHAW, E., *The Hapsburgs* (Weidenfeld and Nicolson, 1971; Corgi, n.e. 1972).

CRANKSHAW, E., *The fall of the House of Hapsburg* (Longman, 1963; Sphere, n.e. 1970).

JASZI, O., *The dissolution of the Hapsburg monarchy* (University of Chicago Press, 1929).

JUDTMANN, F., *Mayerling: the facts behind the legend* (Harrap, 1971).

MACARTNEY, C. A., *Hungary: a short history* (Edinburgh University Press, 1962).

MAY, A. J., *The Hapsburg monarchy, 1867–1914* (O.U.P., 1952).

REDLICH, J., *Emperor Francis Joseph of Austria* (Macmillan, 1929).

TAYLOR, E., *The fall of the Dynasties: the collapse of the old order, 1905–22* (Weidenfeld and Nicolson, 1963).

Germany

ARONSON, T., *The Kaisers* (Cassell, 1971).

BALFOUR, M., *The Kaiser and his times* (Barrie and Jenkins, 1964).

BARKELEY, R., *The Empress Frederick, daughter of Queen Victoria* (Macmillan, 1956).

BENNETT, D., *Vicky: Princess Royal of England and German Empress* (Harvill Press, 1971).

BENSON, E. F., *The Kaiser and his English relations* (Longman, 1936).

BISMARCK, Prince Otto von, *Reflections and reminiscences,* edited by T. S. Hamerow (Harper and Row, 1968).

BISMARCK, Prince Otto von, *Love letters,* edited by Prince Herbert Bismarck, 2 vols (Heinemann, 1901).

CORTI, Count Egon, *The English Empress* (Cassell, 1957).

COWLES, V., *The Kaiser* (Collins, 1963).

FREDERICK III, Emperor of Germany, *Diaries,* edited by M. von Poschinger (Chapman, 1901).

HOWARD, M., *The Franco–Prussian War* (Hart-Davis, 1961).

PAGET, Lady Walpurga, *Scenes and memories* (E. Smith, 1912).

TAYLOR, A. J. P., *Bismarck* (Hamish Hamilton, 1955; New American Library, 1968).

VICTORIA, Empress of Germany, *Letters,* edited by Sir Frederick Ponsonby (Macmillan, 1928).

WILLIAM II, Emperor of Germany, *My early life* (Methuen, 1926).

Russia

ALEXANDRA, Tsaritsa, *Letters of the Tsaritsa to the Tsar, 1914–16,* edited by Sir Bernard Pares (Duckworth, 1923).

ALMEDINGEN, E. M. von, *The Empress Alexandra, 1872–1918* (Hutchinson, 1961).

CHARQUES, R., *The twilight of Imperial Russia* (O.U.P., reissued 1965).

COWLES, V., *The Russian dagger* (Collins, 1969).

DEUTSCHER, I., *The prophet armed: Leon Trotsky, 1879–1921* (O.U.P., n.e. 1970).

FISCHER, L., *The life of Lenin* (Weidenfeld and Nicolson, 1965).

GAPON, G., *The story of my life* (Chapman and Hall, 1905).

KERENSKY, A. T., *The Kerensky memoirs* (Cassell, 1966).

KNOX, Gen. Sir Alfred, *With the Russian army, 1914–17,* 2 vols (Hutchinson, 1921).

KOCHAN, L., *Russia in revolution* (Weidenfeld and Nicolson, 1967; Paladin, 1970).

KRUPSKAYA, N., *Memories of Lenin* (Lawrence and Wishart, rev. edn. 1970; Panther, 1970).

KSCHESSINSKA, M., *Dancing in Petersburg* (Gollancz, 1960).

LOCKHART, R. H. Bruce, *Memories of a British Agent* (Putnam, 1934).

MASSIE, R. K., *Nicholas and Alexandra* (Gollancz, 1968; Pan, 1968).

MOOREHEAD, A., *The Russian Revolution* (Collins, 1958).

MOSOLOV, A. A., *At the Court of the last Tsar* (Methuen, 1935).

NICHOLAS II, Tsar, *The letters of Tsar Nicholas and Empress Marie,* edited by E. J. Bing (Nicholson and Watson, 1937).

PARES, Sir Bernard, *The fall of the Russian monarchy* (Cape, 1939).

RADZIWILL, Princess Catherine, *The intimate life of the last Tsarina* (Cassell, 1929).

RADZIWILL, Princess Catherine, *Nicholas II, the last of the Tsars* (Cassell, 1931).

REED, J., *Ten days that shook the world* (Lawrence and Wishart, 1962; Penguin Books, 1970).

RODZIANKO, M. V., *The reign of Rasputin* (A. M. Philpot, 1927).

SOLZHENITSYN, A., *August 1914* (Bodley Head, 1972).

TROTSKY, L., *The history of the Russian Revolution* (Gollancz, 1965; Sphere, 1970).

WILSON, C., *Rasputin and the fall of the Romanovs* (A. Barker, 1964).

WITTE, Count Sergei, *Memoirs,* edited by A. Yarmolinsky (Heinemann, 1921).

WOLFE, B. D., *Three who made a Revolution* (Thames and Hudson, 1956; Penguin Books, n.e. 1966).

YOUSSOUPOV, Prince Felix, *Rasputin* (Cape, 1927).